Manual of Instructions for Using the Gottschalk-Gleser Content Analysis Scales: Anxiety, Hostility, and Social Alienation– Personal Disorganization

Manual of Instructions for Using the Gottschalk-Gleser Content Analysis Scales: Anxiety, Hostility, and Social Alienation– Personal Disorganization

by Louis A. Gottschalk, M.D.
Carolyn N. Winget, M.A.
Goldine C. Gleser, Ph.D.

University of California Press
Berkeley and Los Angeles 1969

University of California Press
Berkeley and Los Angeles, California
University of California Press, Ltd.
London, England
Copyright © 1969 by The Regents of the University of California
Library of Congress Catalog Card Number: 69-15828
Printed in the United States of America

CONTENTS

I. Relevance of Content Analysis to Other Sciences	1
II. The Preparation of Different Kinds of Verbal Communication for Coding	4
Verbal Samples Obtained by the "Standard" Procedure	5
Obtaining verbal samples	5
Preparing verbal samples for coding	10
Word counts and correction factors	12
Verbal Behavior Obtained from Psychotherapeutic and Other Interviews	15
Dreams	15
Projective Test Materials	15
Other Materials	16
III. Training Technicians for Coding and Scoring Content	17
Useful Learning Techniques	17
Word Count and Reliability of Scores	20
IV. Tabulation and Computation of Final Scores	21
Affect Scales	21
The Social Alienation–Personal Disorganization Scale	22
V. General Rules for All Content Analysis Scales	23
The Coding Unit	23
The Contextual Unit	24
The Summarizing Unit	25
Coding Pronouns as Referents	26
Number of Scores per Clause	27
Grammatical Tense of Clauses	27
Scoring of Dreams, Wishes, and Other Fantasy Material	27
Minimizing Inferences	28
Coding of Generalized Others	28
VI. The Anxiety Scale	29
Introduction	29
Rules for Use	32
Examples	35
Death Anxiety	35
Mutilation Anxiety	38

Separation Anxiety	40
Guilt Anxiety	45
Shame Anxiety	49
Diffuse or Nonspecific Anxiety	52
Verbal Samples and Tabulation Coded for Anxiety	54
VII. The Hostility Directed Outward Scale	**62**
Introduction	62
Rules for Use	65
Examples	67
Overt Hostility Outward	67
Covert Hostility Outward	75
Verbal Samples and Tabulation Coded for Hostility Directed Outward	86
VIII. The Hostility Directed Inward Scale	**93**
Introduction	93
Rules for Use	95
Examples	97
Verbal Samples and Tabulation Coded for Hostility Directed Inward	107
IX. The Ambivalent Hostility Scale	**114**
Introduction	114
Rules for Use	115
Examples	117
Verbal Samples and Tabulation Coded for Ambivalent Hostility	122
X. The Social Alienation–Personal Disorganization (Schizophrenic) Scale	**128**
Introduction	128
Rules for Use	131
Examples	132
Interpersonal References	132
Intrapersonal References	141
References to Disorganization and Repetition	153
Verbal Samples and Tabulation Coded for Social Alienation–Personal Disorganization	158
Bibliography	171
Index of Authors	173
Index of Subjects	173

CHAPTER I
Relevance of Content Analysis to Other Sciences

This manual has been designed to supplement the book *The Measurement of Psychological States Through the Content Analysis of Verbal Behavior* (Gottschalk and Gleser, 1969). Before proceeding to discuss how to use our content analysis scales, let us provide a brief orientation of the relevance of our type of content analysis to linguistics and to the behavioral, social, and medical sciences.

The process of communication is an essential aspect of all social interaction, ranging from the interpersonal to the international levels. Hence, it has been analyzed and studied from many viewpoints. Our own interest has focused on the lexical or verbal features of communication. As such, this content analysis procedure is concerned with verbal communication of symbols or signs and, therefore, falls within the linguistic branch called *semiotics*. Moreover, from the linguistic standpoint, it involves itself with the relationship of (word) signs to signs (syntactics), the relationship of signs to referents (semantics), and the relationship of the sender to the sign (pragmatics) and the sign to the sender (pragmatics).

Quantification is one of the important attributes of our system of content analysis. But it has qualitative as well as quantitative elements. For example, different kinds of emotions and subcategories of emotion can be specified. Also, this content analysis method is not limited to manifest content, that is, to the surface meaning of the content. It aims, also, to analyze the latent content, that is, the deeper layers of meaning embedded in the content.

Earlier definitions of content analysis have tended to limit its denotation to the relationship of signs to signs (syntactics) and of signs to referents (semantics) (Kaplan, 1943; Janis, 1949; Berelson, 1952). There was formerly a reluctance to include in the definition of content analysis the relationship of signs to the people that produce or receive them (pragmatics) because of the difficulty of drawing valid inferences directly from content data about the causes or effects of communication. In our work the validity of these inferences, insofar as they involve the relationship of the sender to his messages, has been checked in a wide variety of validation studies (Gottschalk and Gleser, 1969) for each of the scales discussed in this manual.

Recent trends with regard to the definition of content analysis have been in the direction of a broader definition (Cartwright, 1953; Barcus, 1959; Osgood, 1959; Dunphy, 1964; Marsden, 1965; Holsti, 1967). We subscribe to the very broad definition proposed by Holsti (1967): "Content analysis is any technique for systematically and objectively identifying specified characteristics of messages."

Since we have been interested in measuring psychological states inferable from the content of communication, our type of content analysis has been classified (Marsden, 1965) as belonging to the pragmatic dimension of language studies. Although in most respects our approach to content analysis fits this classification, particularly in that it involves inferences about the relationship of the sender to the sign, in some respects it does not strictly follow the pragmatic model, for it includes attention to syntax and semantics. In other ways, there are some aspects of our system which defy neat compartmentalization, and hence we are presently designating it as an eclectic approach. These details are discussed in the companion book by Gottschalk and Gleser (1969) and will not be elaborated on further here.

The primary purpose of this manual is to provide clear-cut, step-by-step instructions for preparing different kinds of verbal communications for coding and scoring according to five of the content analysis scales we have developed. The scales to be discussed here are four affect scales (Anxiety Scale, Hostility Directed Outward Scale, Hostility Directed Inward Scale, Ambivalently Directed Hostility Scale) and the scale for measuring severity of Social Alienation–Personal Disorganization, also called the "Schizophrenic" Scale. The development of key concepts and theoretical constructs underlying these scales and normative data, generalizability, reliability, and validity are described in the book by Gottschalk and Gleser (1969) and will not be repeated here.

While we have formulated working concepts of the affects or psychological states we are studying, these have not been so rigidly formulated that modifications could not be made of concepts and relevant assumptions, especially when convincing empirical data have been found or new and persuasive theoretical viewpoints have arisen. Thus, our concepts have been constantly under scrutiny; they have expanded here, have contracted there, or have been considerably altered at other points. To the extent that this will continue to be true, this manual can only represent a static orientation to what is in reality a theoretical framework in a constant state of investigation and modification.

A separate section has been devoted to each of the major steps involved in obtaining, preparing, and analyzing verbal samples. The section dealing with each of the five scales includes the scale, specific rules for use of the scale, numerous examples of the range of verbal behavior covered by subcategories of the scale, tabulation techniques, and examples of coded verbal samples.

CHAPTER II
The Preparation of Different Kinds of Verbal Communication for Coding

These content analysis scales can be applied to different kinds of language material obtained in a variety of situations and in both spoken and written form. Most of our reliability and validity studies have been done on short samples of speech, three to five minutes in duration, obtained in response to standard instructions. The instructions have been purposely relatively ambiguous and unstructured with respect to the content to be elicited, except that a report of personal experiences has been requested. We were led to use such instructions because of our initial aim to probe the immediate emotional reactions of our interviewees and to minimize reactions of guarding or covering up. We settled on standardized instructions, also, in order to compare individuals in a standard context so that demographic and personality variables could be explored and investigated while holding relatively constant the influence of such variables as the instructions for eliciting speech (or writing), the interviewer, the context, and the situation. It was our intention to pursue later the effects of varying these noninterviewee variables, one by one, after reliable and valid content analysis scales were developed. We have recently done a number of studies investigating the effects of these noninterviewee variables on the verbal messages produced by interviewees and have turned up some interesting findings. These suggest that the personality of the interviewer, the nature of the method eliciting the verbal behavior, and the situations in which it is evoked influence the verbal content of the message sender (Gottschalk and Gleser, 1969).

Here we will enumerate the different kinds of language materials to which our content analysis scales can be applied, and we will describe, where pertinent, how to obtain these verbal samples and how best to prepare them for content analysis by our procedure.

Much of what follows in this and subsequent chapters of this manual is offered as guidelines to the research assistants, content analysis technicians, secretaries, as well as to principal investigators who intend to use this content analysis procedure. Hence, the text is geared to a broad level of comprehension.

VERBAL SAMPLES OBTAINED BY THE "STANDARD" PROCEDURE

Obtaining verbal samples

STANDARDIZED INSTRUCTIONS

The instructions used in the standardized method of eliciting verbal samples are typed on a 3 × 5 card and are read aloud to the subject prior to turning on the tape recorder. They read:

> This is a study of speaking and conversational habits. Upon a signal from me I would like you to speak for five minutes about any interesting or dramatic personal life experiences you have had. Once you have started I will be here listening to you but I would prefer not to reply to any questions you may feel like asking me until the five-minute period is over. Do you have any questions you would like to ask me now before we start? Well, then, you may begin.

These instructions are designed to simulate roughly a projective test situation or the psychoanalytic interview. The lack of verbal responsiveness of the examiner during the period the subject is speaking, plus a conscious attempt on the part of the examiner to keep at a minimum any nonverbal cues that might indicate his reactions to the subject, tend to give the examiner and the total situation the quality of a "blank screen" on which the subject projects some part of the gamut of his reactions to any vaguely similar life situations within his past experience.

Presumably, what the subject talks about during any one verbal sample depends in part on what psychological conflicts and feelings are being most prominently experienced at that time, that is, what feelings and conflicts are most highly aroused and focal at the moment. This psychological state determines how the subject perceives the experimental situation and of what events from his remote or recent past he is reminded. The standardized nature of the situation in which the verbal samples are elicited minimizes the interviewer as a variable influencing the interviewee's subjective state and speech (that is, the interviewer as a variable influencing change in the message sender is kept relatively constant) and leaves the interviewee's reactions (appropriate and inappropriate) as a predominant variable in the interpersonal interaction.

Since the role of the examiner or observer in obtaining verbal samples is a minimal one, it is not necessary that a professionally trained person read the standardized instructions and operate the tape recorder. A technical assistant who has no other administrative, psychotherapeutic, medical, or other type of role vis-à-vis the subject can administer the procedure necessary in obtaining verbal samples. To date, we have no direct evidence which would indicate that it is necessary to take into consideration the training of the individual who elicits the verbal behavior in order to make it useful and valid as data. The introduction of a technician in obtaining the speech samples instead of the subject's medical physician, psychiatrist, psychologist, or other professional person does not interfere in any discernible way with the validity and reliability of the scores obtained from verbal samples, *provided that the verbal samples in a particular study are all taken by the same person.*

A large literature attests to the effect of the interviewer on subject responses in more structured situations. Certainly such factors as the degree of acquaintanceship or friendship between interviewer and subject can be expected to have an unknown relationship to the amount of defensiveness or openness the subject might feel in choosing and discarding topics to be discussed in a five-minute period. We have evidence that the personality and sex of the interviewer vis-à-vis the subject can have an effect on the overall level of affect scores obtained (Gottschalk and Gleser, 1969), but it is difficult to distinguish between the effects of sex differences and other personality differences.

In addition to the sex of the interviewer, the social status, race, and age are personality factors which should be considered and as far as possible controlled. The best policy to reduce variance due to interviewer effects seems to be the use of a single interviewer to obtain the data on any one subject during longitudinal studies and for all subjects in cross-sectional studies.

EQUIPMENT

A tape recorder, a stop watch, a table, and two chairs constitute minimal equipment. A poor tape recording, which is nevertheless transcribed to a typescript and used for research data, introduces an unnecessary source of unreliability in the results. Persons taking verbal samples must be well instructed in the use of the particular tape recorder(s) that are utilized. Prior to the entrance of the subject the condition of the tape and the tape recorder is checked to make sure that all is in working order, to ascertain the tape speed to be used, the level of sound necessary for adequate recording, and the proper position of the microphone. A unidirectional microphone is often better for recording verbal samples, for an omnidirectional one tends to pick up many otherwise unnoticed background noises which make transcription of the tape difficult.

THE ENVIRONMENT IN WHICH THE VERBAL SAMPLE IS TAKEN

Since verbal samples may be obtained in hospital settings, classrooms, offices, prisons, and so forth, the setting for audiorecording of speech may not always be ideal. If at all possible, however, the equipment should be set up in a room in which no people will be present other than the subject and the examiner. Consideration is given to eliminating as many background noises as possible: air conditioners, electric fans, sounds of typing, talking, laughing from adjacent rooms. Interruptions from telephone calls or visitors are detrimental to the quality of the verbal sample and constitute a distraction to the speaker.

When procuring verbal samples from nonambulatory hospitalized patients, it is frequently possible to gain relative privacy for the necessary five-minute period by requesting that other patients leave the room temporarily or by removing the patient to a separate room. Hospital personnel should be alerted to the importance of an uninterrupted five-minute period.

We have found it feasible to obtain verbal samples via longdistance telephone in instances where the subject's speech has previously been recorded and, hence, where the speaker has some understanding as to what is expected. Special techniques are necessary for this and it is helpful to have a stenographer on a separate extension listening and recording in shorthand so that one need not rely solely on what may be a very uneven and poor tape recording. Since the subject cannot see the tape recorder, it is important to make explicit the request for permission to record the five-minute verbal sample obtained by telephone.

IDENTIFICATION DATA

It is not possible to stress too strongly the importance of adequate identification for all verbal samples. This identification should appear both on the tape recording and on a handwritten list to be given to the stenographer making the transcription. The following is a minimum list of items which are recorded by the examiner prior to the start of the five-minute recording by the subject:

(*a*) Date of recording;
(*b*) Time of day;
(*c*) Name or code number of subject;
(*d*) Name of interviewer.

In addition, we have required that those involved in any type of collection of verbal samples provide us with basic demographic data about the subject, such as age, sex, race, amount of education, and the nature of the sample from which the subject was drawn: college fraternity, student nurse, state mental hospital, hypertension clinic, etc. Very often, the design of the particular study for which the verbal sample is being collected calls for the addition of unique data to the records: drugs administered, hypnotic state present or absent, before or after some experimental procedure, diagnostic category, and so forth. In studies involving experimental variations, it is of special importance that careful notes on the experimental conditions be kept and made a part of the record. Where it is of consequence that such data *not* be available to those who score the verbal sample, it is possible to devise simple codes for the various conditions, the key to each code being kept in a sealed envelope until it is needed for analysis of data after coding and tabulating have been carried out.

RECOMMENDED BEHAVIOR OF PERSON ELICITING
AND COLLECTING VERBAL SAMPLES

Even when the subject claims he has nothing to say, we feel it is necessary to allow for the entire five-minute recording time. Whether the subject continues to talk for the entire five minutes or is mute for a portion of the time, it is our practice to continue sitting, silently if necessary, until the stop watch indicates the five minutes are completed, before turning off the tape recorder and letting the subject know that the recording session is over. Also, interviewers using the standard instructions are advised to keep their facial expression immobile and to sit relatively motionless, so that the speaker is not inadvertently cued on what to say.

While a psychotherapist, physician, or other professional person taking a verbal sample may wish to discuss the content of the sample given, nonprofessional technicians are trained to bring the interview to an immediate close after thanking the subject for participating in the study.

MODIFICATIONS IN THE STANDARD PROCEDURE

In some studies, especially those of a longitudinal nature, where repeated verbal samples are to be given by the same subject, some modification in the above procedures has been used. Obviously, with the average type of subject, it is not necessary to read completely the standardized instructions on numerous occasions. We have found that excellent verbal samples in longitudinal studies can be obtained by placing the tape recorders at the disposal of a subject in his home or office and allowing him to tape his own samples at regular prearranged times without the presence or assistance of an observer (see, for example, Gottschalk et al., 1962). The subject can be told to talk about any topics or feelings he cares to (that is, to free-associate) for five minutes. In such situations, it is advisable to give the subject a card to read aloud at the beginning of each verbal sample so that each sample can later be correctly identified. Such a card might read: "This is subject ———; the date is ———; the time is ———."

We do not know whether the content of verbal samples obtained without the presence of an observer differ in any significant way from those obtained by a trained technician. We suspect there may well be some subtle differences. Colby (1960) has provided some evidence that there may be differences, for he reported fewer references were made to other people when individuals tape-recorded their speech with no one else present as compared to speaking in someone's presence. Hence, it is considered best not to vary these conditions within the same study, so that one does not introduce still another source of variance into what is frequently an all too lengthy list of variables that may influence the content of communications.

Preparing verbal samples for coding

Since the typed transcript of the verbal sample is of primary significance in verbal behavior research, its accuracy is of extreme importance to the reliability and validity of the results. The following procedures are followed in the preparation of typescripts.

a. Preparation of a rough draft of transcript:

1. Include all partial words, stutters, break-offs, and nonverbal vocalizations (e.g., "uh" or "ah").
2. Nonverbal sounds, such as coughs, crying, laughing, etc., are indicated in parentheses at the appropriate point in the typescript.
3. Short pauses are indicated by the word "pause" written in parentheses.
4. Long pauses are indicated by inserting the words "long pause" in parentheses at the appropriate place.
5. Suggested procedures for words that cannot be heard clearly:

   (*a*) Remove earphones and attempt to distinguish words by playing the sound directly to the room at large.

   (*b*) Vary the volume. Words sometimes become more easily distinguishable at a lower or higher volume.

   (*c*) Use a second person to listen.

   (*d*) When all else fails, *do not guess.* Try to determine how many words are being omitted. Indicate the approximate number of words omitted in parentheses at the appropriate point in the transcript.

   (*e*) Ask the person who took the verbal sample for assistance. Especially if the word or phrase is difficult to perceive because of the use of unusual names or words, or odd sentence construction, the investigator who obtained the verbal sample can frequently be helpful.

b. While in rough draft form, the verbal sample is relistened to by an independent observer to check its accuracy. This step is especially crucial for those verbal samples where many nonverbal vocalizations have been used or where there has been difficulty with indistinct words.

c. In general, the total word count and the determination of the proper correction factor can be made from the rough draft at this point in the procedure. This ensures that all final copies of the verbal sample will carry this necessary information. (See next section for instructions for counting words and determining correction factors.)

  d. Final typing:

  1. Number of copies.—Since at least two independent scorings are ordinarily made of each verbal sample, and frequently several different scales are utilized, an adequate number of easily readable copies is prepared in the final typing. With an electric typewriter, it has been found that up to ten copies can be made, the first on white bond and subsequent copies on onion skin. Other methods of duplicating, such as the ditto process, may also be used.

  2. Heading.—The heading on the first page of each verbal sample contains the following information:

  (*a*) Name of the subject or appropriate code number to be repeated on continuation pages);

  (*b*) Date and time;

  (*c*) Name of study;

  (*d*) Name of the observer or technician who took the verbal sample;

  (*e*) Total word count;

  (*f*) Correction factor;

  (*g*) On controlled experimental studies, a code word may also be included in the heading indicative of the experimental condition. The key to the code is then kept by the research secretary in a sealed envelope until such time as it is needed for data analysis.

  3. Spacing.—All verbal samples are preferably typed *triple-spaced* in final form so as to allow sufficient space between lines for easy coding.

  4. Breaking up the verbal sample into coding units.—In order to be sure that the unit coded—in this instance the grammatical clause—is the same for all technicians, we have for several years followed a procedure of breaking the verbal sample into clauses before the final transcript is reproduced. With the use of the ditto masters for the final copy, this process is quite simple. A knowledgeable person determines the clauses, using diagonal marks to indicate them on the ditto master after the typing is completed but prior to its being duplicated. In cases where carbon copies are utilized as the final copies, it is probably preferable that the clauses be demarcated on the rough draft for in-

corporation as part of the final typing. In any event, it has been our experience (in view of difficulties in delineating clauses with multiple predicate, dangling phrases, or clauses contained within clauses) that it is time-saving and convenient for the scorers if the material to be coded has already been broken into units by one person.

A discussion on identifying the unit to be scored is included in the section on general rules applicable to all the scales (Chapter V).

Word counts and correction factors

The following rules are used in counting the number of words contained in any verbal sample. The count is used to obtain a correction factor applicable to the raw frequency scores of any of the content scales subsequently coded. Use of the correction factor makes possible the comparison of scores derived from speech samples of varying length.

RULES FOR COUNTING WORDS BY HAND

1. Such fill words as "er," "uh," etc., are included on the rough typescript but are not counted and are not included in our final typescript.

2. Numbers indicating the time of day, year, measurement, age, or such designations as the title of a regiment or street are counted as one word.

Examples

Time of day:	4:35 (1 word) P.M. (1 word)
Year:	1963 (1 word)
Measurement:	5,333 (1 word)
	1,000,000 (1 word)
	2 and $\frac{1}{2}$: 2 (1 word) and (1 word)
	$\frac{1}{2}$ (1 word) = (3 words)
Age:	18 years old (3 words)
Title of regiment or other military unit:	
	108th (1 word) Airborne (1 word)
Street numbers:	1031 (1 word) 44th Street (2 words)

3. Contractions are counted as one word.
    Examples: I'll, we're, it's, you're, he's
4. The proper name of a person is counted as one word.

However, while a name such as "Mary Jane Smith" is counted as one word, rather than three, if it is preceded by a title of some sort (e.g., Mrs., Mr., Miss, Doctor, General, President, Professor, etc.), the title is counted as a separate word. Thus, Mrs. Mary Jane Smith would be counted as two words.

5. Proper nouns designating places are generally counted as one word. Examples: New York, Los Angeles, San Francisco, Grand Canyon, YMCA. However, generic terms used in conjunction with proper-noun designations are counted separately—for example, Good Samaritan Hospital (2 words); Gibson Hotel (2 words); New York Railway (2 words).

6. Some hyphenated words, such as semi-clad, are counted as two words.

7. All interjections are counted. Examples: Oh, gee, gee whiz (two words), golly, etc.

8. The names of companies containing more than one word are given a count equal to the number of words; for example, General Electric Company equals three words.

9. When "a while" is used as a noun it is counted as two words, whereas when it is used as an adverb, "awhile," it is counted as one word. Example: "Let us rest here a while." In this statement, "a while" is two words, the word "while" being used as a noun to indicate a space of time. However, in a statement such as "He left here awhile ago," the "awhile" is given an adverbial use and counted as one word.

SUGGESTIONS FOR COUNTING WORDS WITH ELECTRIC COUNTERS

It is not difficult to attach an electronic counter to electric typewriters so that words are automatically counted during the final typing of the verbal sample. A few simple suggestions or rules to be followed by the typist will yield a verbal sample word count which is quite reliable.

1. Since the electronic counter records one word each time the space bar is pressed, it is important to use single spaces after sentences.

2. There are two possibilities for the word at the end of a line. One is to get in the habit of adding a space before returning the carriage. The other is to ignore the spaces at the end of lines until the verbal sample is completed and then count the number of lines and add one space for each to the total. (Be sure to add

a space for the last line on the page, which may only be a partial line.)

3. Partial or incomplete words are counted.

4. All fills (uhs, ahs) and indications of nonverbal behavior (laughs, coughs, crying, etc.), as well as interviewer remarks, are omitted on the final typescript. Where their inclusion is of some importance in the use to be made of the verbal sample, the electronic counter is switched off so that words not properly part of the verbal sample are not counted.

5. Contractions count for one word.

6. Names of companies, people, etc.—Use hyphens instead of spaces between such designations as Joe-Smith or the Blue-Bell-Company.

7. Words omitted.—The word count should include the estimated number of omitted words. The typist may type the number of missing words in the typescript in such a way that the electronic counter will register the number of missing words. We suggest inserting extra spaces (registered by the electronic counter as words) minus two spaces before a closing parenthesis in the following manner:

(*a*) one word: I went to (word) in the country;
(*b*) two words: I wanted to buy a (2 words) for my sister;
(*c*) three words: I couldn't find the (3 words omitted);
(*d*) 4 words or more: I wanted to buy a (4 words   ) for my sister;
(*e*) 1 sentence: (6 words   ). That is, 6 less 2 spaces between "words" and close parenthesis.

CORRECTION FACTOR

The correction factor for each verbal sample is determined by the formula:

$$\frac{1}{\text{Number of words}} \times 100$$

Either a calculator or a conversion table is ordinarily used in determining the correction factor.

VERBAL BEHAVIOR OBTAINED FROM PSYCHOTHERAPEUTIC AND OTHER INTERVIEWS

These content analysis procedures can be applied to interview material, psychotherapeutic, diagnostic, or otherwise. Our principal applications to interviews have involved psychotherapeutic interviews (Gottschalk et al., 1961, 1966a). The mechanics of applying our verbal behavior method are similar, regardless of the type of interview.

The typed data can be broken down into equal temporal units (for example, two- or five-minute segments). Or the units can be based on the number of words spoken by one or both participants (or more if they are present); for example, consecutive 500-word sequences of a speaker or speakers can be coded for content, depending on the purpose and research design of a study.

DREAMS

The application of these content analysis scales to dreams has been carried out in a number of studies (see, for example, Witkin et al., 1965; Karacan et al., 1966; Gottschalk et al., 1966b; Winget, 1967). In these studies, the content analysis was applied to the report of the dream itself and not to the dreamer's associations to the dream content. An investigator could, however, apply our scales to the free associations stemming from the dreams, and, according to the investigator's theoretical predilection, the scores obtained from the dream associations could be examined separately from or in combination with the scores derived from the actual dream. We recommend using only dreams (or any verbal samples) of at least 70 or more words because the smaller the number of words in the verbal sample, the less the adequacy or reliability of the sample as a true measure of any psychological variable. Dream reports consisting of more than, say, 100 words would provide an even more reliable estimate of some psychological state, but a choice of a minimum of 70 words has been arrived at as a rough compromise between reliability of sampling and loss of research data.

PROJECTIVE TEST MATERIALS

Projective test data, specifically tape recordings of TAT responses (Murray, 1943), have served as verbal behavior data to which our content analysis scales have been applied (Gottschalk and Hambidge, 1955; Gottschalk and Gleser, 1969).

Because of the very nature of a projective test, such as the TAT, direct references to the self experiencing some emotion or drive are not made by the speaker and, hence, these thematic content categories are not available for scoring. Therefore, a total score for any of our content analysis scales on TAT stories does not include that portion stemming from direct references involving the self. Nevertheless, this does not appear to constitute a crucial loss of information with respect to the capacity of the scales to distribute the content of TAT protocols on a quantitative dimension comparable with other methods of scoring. For instance, hostility outward scores were obtained independently from TAT protocols (Gottschalk et al., 1963), using the method of Hafner and Kaplan (1960), as well as by one of our nonprofessional technicians using the Gottschalk-Gleser hostility outward scale; the rank-order correlation was 0.72 ($p < .01$). Furthermore, we have found that our scale of social alienation–personal disorganization applied to TAT protocols obtained from schizophrenic patients and their families significantly differentiated the schizophrenic individuals from the nonschizophrenic members of each family.

We have usually scored TAT protocols by obtaining a separate score from each card and then averaging to obtain the final score. When this is done, the number of words in each story must be obtained separately. Elsewhere (Gottschalk and Gleser, 1969) we have provided evidence that the consistency among TAT cards when scoring psychological states is satisfactory using this method.

OTHER MATERIALS

The application of these content analysis scales has been applied, with meaningful results, to written verbal samples (Ross et al., 1963; Gottschalk and Gleser, 1969). To increase the adequacy of sampling, we now recommend that written verbal samples elicited by means of our standard instructions be at least ten minutes in length, rather than only five minutes.

Application of these scales to literature, letters, public speeches, and any other type of language material is quite feasible. The validity of the conclusions drawn from such applications are, as in all scientific research, dependent on the adequacy of the research design, the controls, the methods of statistical evaluation of the data, and all other relevant aspects of the scientific method.

CHAPTER III
Training Technicians for Coding and Scoring Content

In the development of thematic content scales for scoring verbal material, we have paid considerable attention to the consistency of scores obtained by different technicians using our scales. Such concern reflects our aim to develop content categories which are as clearly defined as possible, so that scoring might be objective rather than intuitive and idiosyncratic and might be based on literal rather than figurative assessment of content. Moreover, since our investigations have been continuing over a number of years, it has been necessary to insure comparability of scores obtained at different periods and with different scoring technicians.

A variety of techniques may be used in the training of research technicians to ensure comprehension and proper use of these verbal behavior scales. This manual contains sections devoted to general assumptions which underlie all the scales, general rules applicable to all the scales, and carefully worked out specific rules for the individual scales. While it is not necessary for a content analyst using these scales to be a psychiatrist, psychologist, social scientist, or even necessarily to be psychologically oriented, it is essential that persons trained to code verbal samples have adequate education, intelligence, and motivation to understand and use the assumptions and instructions. It is probably necessary that the scorer have some basic interest and insight into the uses and nuances of language. In addition, some healthy degree of compulsiveness and the capacity to tolerate ambiguity are important attributes.

USEFUL LEARNING TECHNIQUES

A. A careful study of pertinent sections of this manual to insure that the purpose and meaning of the scale to be learned are understood. Considerable attention should be given to fixing in mind the specific rules for the scale to be mastered, as well as achieving a general familiarity with the types of examples provided for the various subcategories of the scale and where they can be located for checking during coding.

B. If a technician is being added to a research team which is already producing verbal samples coded for content, it is helpful to orient the new person by having him begin with the tabulation of the scoring of an experienced coder. This is not a meaningful experience unless the person to be trained really scrutinizes the scoring he is tabulating and feels free to raise questions about uses and ambiguities of the scale which he is learning.

C. Study of previously scored verbal samples is another useful learning method. This involves having the scale before one and checking each scored clause against the scale to verify its applicability. Again, this technique is only useful if the person being trained notes the questions which arise and discusses them with an experienced coder.

D. At some point in the training of a content-analysis technician, self-testing is a useful learning device. The usefulness of this approach depends largely, of course, on the motivation of the technician-in-training. The trainee scores verbal samples not previously studied by him and then checks his scoring with the scoring of others on identical samples to determine discrepancies. If it appears that there is essential agreement, an interjudge reliability correlation is run at this point to determine if the trainee's use of the scale is adequate. Training is considered adequate if the scores obtained on a sample of 30 or more cases correlate at least 0.80 with an experienced coder and if the average scores for the sample are comparable, indicating no bias in the overall application of the scale.

E. Coding conferences are useful to a research team which has been working together for some time as well as to a technician first learning a new scale. All persons to be involved are provided with the same verbal samples which are then independently coded. At the coding conference, each verbal sample is reviewed clause by clause and all differences are thoroughly discussed. Lack of agreement may result from three sources: (1) coding errors; (2) disagreement due to ambiguity of the content to be coded or the content category itself; and (3) improper use of the scale. These sources of variance are discussed below.

1. *Coding errors.*—By "coding error" we mean the overlooking of an obviously codable clause, placing the clause in an inappropriate category when one "knows" it belongs in another; coding the clause in the proper subcategory but designating it incorrectly, as in giving anxiety regarding death to the self a weight of two rather than three, etc. An analogy would be the type of simple arithmetic errors one may make even when quite familiar with the mathematical process involved. Some technicians make more of these kinds of errors than do others, and the same technician may vary from time to time in the number of such errors made. Usually the tendency to make this type of error will diminish if the matter is brought to the attention of the technician and more time is given to reviewing each verbal sample after it has been coded.

2. *Disagreement due to ambiguity.*—Coding conferences will help to clarify the different interpretations placed on any one specific clause and the contextual unit in which it is embedded. Given the complexities of the English language, one hopes that through detailed discussion of ambiguous areas, the amount of disagreement can be reduced, if not eliminated, as to whether statements made by a message sender are properly coded in one content category or another. To the extent that such ambiguity revolves around subcategories with equal weights, the total score assigned to a verbal sample will not be affected by the differences in scoring. However, if the disagreement involves the issue of whether a clause is, indeed, scorable or not, interscorer reliability may be reduced if satisfactory rules for making such discriminations cannot be spelled out. The safest rule here seems to be to resolve such disagreements by having technicians underscore rather than overscore content of this type.

3. *Errors due to improper use of the scales.*—Errors of this type tend to drop out as the trainee becomes more thoroughly oriented and knowledgeable about the rules, examples, and meaning of the scales. Even the well-trained technician, however, may make errors of this kind after some years of coding. Sometimes this is due to temporary shifts in attitudes. For example, one technician who had recently lost a family member due to cancer found herself deciding that all references to cancer in verbal samples necessarily conveyed the message that the speaker was experiencing death anxiety. A coder who customarily added correctly the

additional weight for verbalized intensity when using the Anxiety Scale (i.e., when a codable statement includes an adjective or adverb modifier which, itself, denotes greater magnitude) may, for no obvious reason, be found to be using the scale as though this rule for augmenting the weight assigned to such a content item did not exist. We are aware that the psychological state of the coder can influence the way a verbal sample is scored in much the same way that the countertransference of a psychoanalyst may influence the objectivity of his perception and the response to a patient. Periodic checking is necessary for all coding technicians of a research team to ensure that such biases are made explicit and discussed. Our method of tabulating allows for easy inspection of the use of the various subcategories to see whether some categories are consistently over- or underused vis-à-vis the coding of others.

It is useful to have trainees work with a wide variety of types of verbal samples during training so as to ensure consistency of coding for different research projects. There is, for example, a tendency for the person who has utilized the Schizophrenic Scale only on the verbal behavior of chronic schizophrenics to utilize the scale in subtly different ways when it is known that verbal samples being scored were produced by nonschizophrenic individuals.

In psychophysiological and psychobiochemical studies, we have adopted the routine of using the average of two independent scores for all our data, for this elevates the reliability of the final score. More detailed information on scoring reliability is available in the companion book by Gottschalk and Gleser (1969).

WORD COUNT AND RELIABILITY OF SCORES

We recommend using only verbal samples of at least 70 or more words because the smaller the number of words in the verbal sample, the less the adequacy or reliability of the sample as a true measure of any psychological variable. Verbal samples consisting of more than, say, 100 words would provide a more reliable estimate of some psychological state, but a choice of a minimum of 70 words has been arrived at as a rough compromise between reliability of sampling and loss of research data.

CHAPTER IV
Tabulation and Computation of Final Scores

AFFECT SCALES

As can be seen from the scored excerpts of verbal samples included as the final pages of each section dealing with one of the affect scales, the coding contains the identification of the type of reference and the weight. To make for ease of analysis of the data, it has been our practice to tabulate the number of references in each category on summary sheets, the subcategories of the scale serving as column headings and each verbal sample (identified by name or subject number), along with the identifying data and correction factor, arranged on the rows. The score for any particular subcategory is obtained by summing the weights of all the verbal references made within that category during the verbal sample. The total raw score for any affect is then the sum of scores over all categories.

Individuals differ considerably in rate of speech and the same individual may vary in rate from one occasion to another. Since our numerical indices of magnitude of emotion tend to vary with the number of words spoken per unit of time, it is deemed advisable to correct for this verbal-fluency factor. Furthermore, many verbal samples contain no scorable references on one or more scales. Such samples, regardless of their length, would all have a zero score on that scale. Yet less affect is involved in a long sample than in a short one with only one scorable reference. We have finally decided that the most satisfactory and simplest way to take into consideration rate of speech is by adding 0.5 to the raw score obtained on an affect scale, multiplying by one hundred and dividing by the number of words spoken. This method avoids the discontinuity occurring whenever no scorable items have occurred in some verbal samples. It also provides a uniform transformation over all samples, and with rare exceptions reduces the correlation between the affect scores and the number of words essentially to zero.

To reduce skewness, the square root of this ratio is used as the final corrected score. The square-root-ratio score has the advantage of simplicity and greater homogeneity of variance from sample to sample.

To summarize, the mathematical formula we are using to ascertain the magnitude of an affect is:

$$\text{Magnitude of an affect} = \sqrt{\frac{100 \, (f_1 w_1 + f_2 w_2 + f_3 w_3 \ldots f_n w_n + 0.5)}{N}}$$

where f_n is the frequency per unit of time of any relevant type of thematic verbal reference, w_n is the weight applied to such verbal statements, and N is the number of words per unit of time. Operationally, we usually obtain $100/N$ as the first step, and use it as a multiplier of the raw score. This ratio is what we term "the correction factor."

THE SOCIAL ALIENATION–PERSONAL DISORGANIZATION SCALE

The tabulation and computation of final scores obtained from the use of the Social Alienation and Personal Disorganization (or Schizophrenic) Scale differ somewhat from the procedure used for the affect scales as outlined above.

Obtaining a correction factor based on the number of words spoken per unit of time is still a first step. Since this scale may yield either positive or negative scores, however, it is no longer necessary to guard against the discontinuity which may result from zero scores. In addition, of course, one cannot use a square-root transformation for such scores.

In brief, in computing corrected total scores for the schizophrenic scale, one should note that the weight is not an integral part of the coding system used and that zero and positive and negative weighted frequencies are algebraically summed to arrive at the total weighted-frequency score, which is then multiplied by the correction factor.

CHAPTER V
General Rules for All Content Analysis Scales

THE CODING UNIT

The unit to be coded is the clause, whether independent or dependent. Subordinate or dependent clauses are ordinarily those related to the primary clause by such words as "because," "since," "when," "which," "who,' or "that." Dependent clauses may be scored whether they are classified as adverbial, adjective, or noun clauses. It should be noted that a phrase serving to make for a multiple predicate or a multiple subject or object *is not* considered as a separate clause. Where such phrases contain different scorable ideas, the rule is followed of giving the score that indicates the greatest intensity. Instances where either the subject or the predicate is omitted but is understood are considered as scorable clauses.

On those occasions where one must make a decision as to whether there is a missing but understood (elliptical) subject or predicate, or whether a phrase is part of a multiple subject or predicate, differences of opinion can certainly arise. Often, these controversies cannot be simply resolved by consultation with grammarians or English professors, for grammatical rules themselves may permit several alternative solutions to such issues. In any event, we suspect that slight differences in determining clauses arising from such ambiguities will make a relatively small contribution to error variance in the overall score. In our laboratory, however, we have customarily had one person provide the "clausing," thus keeping constant this source of error. We do this by marking the clauses on the "ditto" master prior to running off and distributing the final copies.

The following examples are given to assist in making discriminations with respect to clausing.

Example 1:

And I was outside with the BB gun shooting at cars / and a guy came up and asked me / wh . . . why, wh . . . where I got the BB gun at / and I told him / I found it laying there / so he start taking us in and calling my house and that. /

Example 2:

Now as I feel, / if I could get something, just for a good nerve medicine / like the doctor, he give me some green capsules; / and I been taking them and taking them. /

Example 3:

I lived with my mother, father, and this brother / before we moved sort of in the country / where we had a large plot of land / that our house was on. /

Parenthetical clauses.—A somewhat frequent form of the clause is that which is set off within the limits of another larger clause. These are marked by double diagonal marks, as in the following examples.

Example 1:

The only thing // I want to do // is / after I had the car wreck. /

Example 2:

I seem more close to her // after I had the wreck // now / than I did before. /

Example 3:

I got up at six o'clock / and (I) took her husband to work / and the only reason // they asked me // was / because I had my driver's license. /

Example 4:

But it ain't // you know // to my idea of it. /

Example 5:

There's this ache / I been having for about oh, // I'd say // about six or seven months. /

THE CONTEXTUAL UNIT

It will be obvious from the lists of examples of coded clauses given for each portion of a scale that frequently a wider context than the clause to be scored must be considered in the decision-making process. We have not been able to arrive at any hard and fast rules regarding the limits to which context must be considered. In part, this is due to the variations in the amount of ambiguity present in the verbal behavior of different people. In one person, a scoring decision may be quite easily made on the basis of each individual clause; in another, it may be necessary to take into account the clause immediately preceding and the one immediately following in order to make an appropriate decision about the score. In still other subjects, the entire verbal sample needs to be considered, or relevant material will be omitted in the scoring. The most extreme example of how broad the range may be in considering the context of the unit to be scored is found in those longitudinal studies where the technician may build up quite an intimate knowledge of how the speaker utilizes referents and the meanings he assigns to them. For example, a daily verbal sample may begin with the statement "Well, it really bothered me again today." If one were scoring this clause for anxiety, and no other context were considered, one might assign the clause to the category of diffuse anxiety experienced by the self ($6a3$), giving it an increased weight ($6a4$) to take into account the use of the word "really" as an intensification of the affect present. However, if it is clear from previous verbal samples that the subject is referring to her embarrassment because of two missing front teeth, the proper anxiety category would be the shame category and a score of ($5a4$) would be assigned.

THE SUMMARIZING UNIT

In line with the concepts of "unit to be coded" and "contextual unit" outlined above, we have also followed Dollard and Auld (1959) in specifying various types of "summarizing units." The type of summarizing unit used depends primarily on the nature of the data gathered. Where such data is the standardized five-minute verbal sample, it is, of course, the summarizing unit used. In other instances, however, we have applied the scales for the measurement of affect to the data of the therapeutic hour, to interviews revolving around family interaction, to dreams, to lengthy daily tape recordings of nonspecified length, and to the longer verbal samples called for in some experimental situations. The decision as to what the summarizing unit should be in each of these instances depends upon such factors as research design, the importance of correlating brief changes in affect with other variables that fluctuate over fairly small time units, and so forth. Types of summarizing units which have been used are 500-word segments, dream reports exclusive of elaboration and associations, therapy sessions broken into two- or five-minute time intervals, and the total number of words spoken by individual members during a group interaction setting.

As we have previously indicated, the fewer the words in a verbal sample, the less reliable or representative is the sample as an indicator of the speaker's or writer's current psychological experience. The reliability of a language sample begins to decrease rapidly as the number of words drops under 100. Hence, we are extremely cautious about the implications of psychological scores derived from verbal samples composed of less than 100 words. Even though valuable data may be lost, we recommend that a summarizing unit must contain a minimum of 70 words to be coded for affect.

CODING PRONOUNS AS REFERENTS

Clauses in which a pronoun clearly stands for a previously coded event or experience should be coded similarly. For example, if the clause "They made fun of me," coded 5a3 for shame anxiety experienced by self, were followed by the clause "They've done *that* ever since I can remember," this reference would also be coded 5a3. A difficulty arises, however, in deciding how many succeeding clauses containing pronomial references to a previous clause should be scored. Consider, for example, the following series of clauses, which are to be scored for hostility directed inward (clauses are numbered for discussion below):

                    1   2
. . . and my spirits is not as bad / as *they* used to be. / Of course,
        3   4
they worry me at times / but I try to shoo *them* away. / But I don't
  5
let *them* worry me much. /

In clause 1, the statement is to the effect that current feelings are not so bad. The "they" of clause 2 conveys the idea that formerly there was a time or discouragement and/or depression and is scored IC3 on the Hostility Inward Scale. Clause 3 also seems to refer clearly to feelings of discouragement and/or depression. By clauses 4 and 5, however, one has drifted somewhat from the original statements of spirits being equated with feelings of discouragement-depression, and one might well argue that the concept of worry has intervened as a separate feeling. This drifting away from the original referent of a pronoun occurs fairly frequently in some subjects. Our general advice to content analysts using our scale is to avoid making inferences as to meaning, for these are built into the choice of content categories in our scales and the weights assigned to content items. Follow the literal, rather than the figurative, meaning conveyed, and when in doubt do not code; thus clauses 4 and 5 would not be coded in the above example. Agreement on this rule minimizes interscorer variance.

NUMBER OF SCORES PER CLAUSE

While there are a number of exceptions, as will be noted in the specific rules for each scale, in general only one score is given to each clause when scoring for any specific affect scale, although the same clause may be coded for more than one affect. One notable exception is with the use of the Social Alienation–Personal Disorganization Scale, where, under certain circumstances, several scores may be given to a single clause.

GRAMMATICAL TENSE OF CLAUSES

References to the subcategories of the scales are to be scored regardless of the grammatical tense in which they are expressed; that is, whether expressed in a past, present, or future tense, or expressed in a conditional sense, or whether stated as a wish or hope. One exception to this will be noted in the specific rules accompanying the scale for social alienation and personal disorganization.

SCORING OF DREAMS, WISHES, AND OTHER FANTASY MATERIAL

Reports of dreams, quotations of poetry, songs, or similar material appearing in verbal samples are coded. Thus the statement "I dreamed I was in jail" would be scored as indicating guilt anxiety ($4a3$). If a speaker happened to quote a line from the Shakespeare sonnet "When in disgrace with Fortune and men's eyes . . ." etc., this statement would receive a score indicating guilt anxiety experienced by animate other (4*b*2) unless the speaker clearly indicated in the context that he is applying this sentiment to himself (in which case it would be scored (4*a*3)) rather than merely attributing it to feelings which the poet alone experienced.

MINIMIZING INFERENCES

Since important inferences regarding the emotional state of the speaker are built into the subcategories of the individual scales, it is very important that those using the scale rely as much as possible on the literal or objective content of the language used by the subject. Perhaps the most important rule regarding the amount of inference to be made is: If in doubt as to whether the inference is justified, DO NOT CODE.

CODING OF GENERALIZED OTHERS

There is a tendency in the use of the English language for speakers to use either "one" or "you" to mean both generalized others and/or the self. At times the content and the accompanying context of a clause make it clear that the subject is referring to himself. For example, consider the following assertions: "You work hard and struggle to the best of your ability all your life / and at the end you got nothing / and you die all alone. / This is / how I feel about it." / In this example, one would score the clauses for affect attributed to the self rather than to others.

In other instances, the speaker is more clearly referring to generalized others and the self is not the primary focus. An example might be: "You have to go up a terribly winding road to get there, / and you see the stream running far below." /

The contextual unit for deciding whether "one" or "you" is a reference to the speaker or to generalized others may sometimes include all of the material in the verbal sample up to the point of occurrence of the clause containing the pronoun for which a decision is to be made. On some occasions, the context following the questionable clauses provides the key to the content analyst's dilemma.

CHAPTER VI
The Anxiety Scale

INTRODUCTION

The type of anxiety this scale has been designed to measure might be termed "free" anxiety in contrast to "bound" anxiety, which may manifest itself in the psychological mechanisms of conversion and hypochondriacal symptoms, in compulsions, in doing and undoing, in withdrawal from human relationships, and so forth. It is likely, however, that some aspects of bound anxiety are registered by our scale, particularly by means of those content items in the scale which involve the psychological mechanisms of displacement and denial. So far as we know at this time, such bound anxiety is preconscious, is relatively readily accessible to consciousness, and is capable, along with grossly conscious anxiety feelings, of activating autonomic nervous system and central nervous system signs of arousal. There is evidence, in fact, that our anxiety scores reflect not only the subjective awareness of anxiety from the conscious and the preconscious level, but also the level of relevant autonomic arousal and the level of relevant postural and kinesic activity. It should be noted here that we have not attempted to differentiate between fear and anxiety by means of this anxiety scale, since we believe it is impossible to make such a distinction on the basis of verbal content alone (see Schedule 1).

In our development of a means of quantifying the intensity of anxiety, there has been an attempt to include in this measurement different qualities of anxiety, depending on the context in which the anxiety is being generated. We have classified anxiety, on the basis of clinical experience, into six subtypes: death, mutilation, separation, guilt, shame, and diffuse or nonspecific anxiety. We recognize that the nature and sources of anxiety may be classified in other ways than these and that the categories we are using are not always mutually exclusive, distinctive, or unique. We believe, however, that our way of structuring the components of the general construct of anxiety has proved to be of considerable heuristic and predictive value.

In order to convert our categorical thematic information drawn from verbal statements into a scale that measures the amount of anxiety experienced by the individual in a given interval of time, we have made several assumptions that should be specified.

First, as stated in the general assumptions that underlie all of the scales of immediate affect which we have developed (Gottschalk and Gleser, 1969), we have assumed that statements of a particular type reflect an equivalent amount of current anxiety on the part of the speaker, whether they pertain to feelings or events occurring or potentially occurring in the past, present, or future. Therefore, as will be seen in the lists of examples, we give the same weight to the statement "I was ashamed to be seen doing it" as to the statement "If I had done it, I would be ashamed."

Second, we have assumed that the more anxiety a person is experiencing at a given moment, the greater is the probability that he will speak of incidents in which he reports being directly threatened, provided that he communicates verbally at all. When the anxiety is somewhat less potent, the subject is more likely to express it indirectly by externalization or displacement and, hence, is more likely to speak in terms of others being hurt or in a dangerous situation or, even more remotely, in terms of inanimate objects being injured or destroyed. We therefore give progressively less weight to remarks about the experiences of other persons and about inanimate objects than we do to experiences in which the speaker is directly involved.

One can see, therefore, that our anxiety scale, though classifiable as a "content" scoring system, does not deal simply with obvious expressions of anxiety, since it contains the built-in inferences that statements about others experiencing anxiety or danger are cues to the speaker's own anxieties and that the frequency of such statements is related to the intensity of the experience. Furthermore, spontaneous denials of anxiety are also counted as indicating the probable presence of a low level of anxiety. Some empirical supportive evidence for this hypothesis has been reported by Gottschalk and Gleser (1969, pp. 115–117).

Another assumption specific to our anxiety scale is that the subtypes of anxiety are of equivalent importance and relevance to the magnitude of overall anxiety of the subject and that they are therefore additive. Thus, the weighted scores for all statements falling into the six subtypes mentioned above are summed to obtain a measure of total anxiety.

It should be noted that, since the scale is designed to tap "immediate" anxiety, the scores of an individual may fluctuate considerably from day to day or hour to hour; a single score is not a good indicator of a subject's typical level of anxiety over any extended period of time. The average of five or more such scores suitably spaced, however, does differentiate individuals reliably in this respect.

SCHEDULE 1
Anxiety Scale*

1. Death anxiety—references to death, dying, threat of death, or anxiety about death experienced by or occurring to:
    a. self (3).
    b. animate others (2).
    c. inanimate objects destroyed (1).
    d. denial of death anxiety (1).
2. Mutilation (castration) anxiety—references to injury, tissue, or physical damage, or anxiety about injury or threat of such experienced by or occurring to:
    a. self (3).
    b. animate others (2).
    c. inanimate objects (1).
    d. denial (1).
3. Separation anxiety—references to desertion, abandonment, loneliness, ostracism, loss of support, falling, loss of love or love object, or threat of such experienced by or occurring to:
    a. self (3).
    b. animate others (2).
    c. inanimate objects (1).
    d. denial (1).
4. Guilt anxiety—references to adverse criticism, abuse, condemnation, moral disapproval, guilt, or threat of such experienced by:
    a. self (3).
    b. animate others (2).
    d. denial (1).
5. Shame anxiety—references to ridicule, inadequacy, shame, embarrassment, humiliation, over-exposure of deficiencies or private details, or threat of such experienced by:
    a. self (3).
    b. animate others (2).
    d. denial (1).
6. Diffuse or nonspecific anxiety—references by word (see pp. 60–61) or in phrases to anxiety and/or fear without distinguishing type or source of anxiety:
    a. self (3).
    b. animate others (2).
    d. denial (1).

* Numbers in parentheses are the weights.

Further details of our construct "anxiety," the assumptions underlying this scale, and a review of normative, reliability, and validity studies have been presented elsewhere (Gottschalk and Gleser, 1969).

It will be observed on the Anxiety Scale that an arabic numeral is assigned to each of the subtypes of anxiety-fear; that is, "death anxiety" is labeled 1, "mutilation anxiety" is labeled 2, etc. In addition, under each subtype there is a listing of lower-case letters. In all cases, "*a*" is equated with the self; "*b*" with animate others; "*c*" with inanimate objects; and "*d*" with denial of the affect. The category "*c*" (inanimate objects) is excluded from subtypes 4, 5, and 6 (guilt, shame, and diffuse anxiety, respectively). The arabic numeral placed just after the "self," "animate others," etc., indicates the weight to be given; a scoring symbol of 1*a*3, for example, can be interpreted as "death anxiety experienced by self, weighted three"; or, a symbol of 4*b*2 can be read "guilt anxiety experienced by animate other, weighted two." As mentioned in rule 4 below, if the statement of anxiety or fear is modified to indicate that the condition is extreme, the weight should be increased by one. A statement of the type "I was terribly afraid of being hurt" would therefore be coded 2*a*4, the last digit indicating that a weight of four is assigned to this statement.

RULES FOR THE USE OF THE ANXIETY SCALE[1]

1. A reference in a clause is *not* scored if the speaker is the agent and the injury, criticism, death wish, shame, etc., is directed toward another. This rule is maintained even in those instances where "we" is used as the subject of the clause, indicating that it is the self and others jointly acting as the agent causing the anxiety.

Examples of clauses *not* scored because the speaker is included as an agent of the anxiety:

I hit him.
We really made him feel guilty that time.
Our leaving made him feel pretty lonely and sad.
I guess / we all joined in making fun of him.
There were times / when I wished / he would die.
We worried her so / that it's no wonder / her hair turned gray.

2. When the subject of a clause is "we" or the object is "us," indicating that the self and others are experiencing the anxiety-fear, the clause is scored for the self alone.

---

[1] See also general rules applicable to all scales, p. 23.

Examples:

The teacher made us feel ashamed. (5a3)
We all had bloody noses / before it was over. (2a3)
We thought / the shell had our name on it. (1a3)
The cops chased us all over the park. (4a3)
We were worried about it. (6a3)

3. Consistent with the approach that this scale does not attempt to differentiate between anxiety and fear, external sources or situations may be the causal factor of the anxiety in any of the six subcategories.

Examples:

The storm tore the branches from the trees. (2c1)
He threatened to kill me. (1a3)
They locked me up in a closet. (3a3)
I was threatened with a court suit. (4a3)

4. The weight given a codable anxiety clause is always increased by one point if the statement of anxiety or fear is modified to indicate that the condition is marked or extreme. While intensity is ordinarily indicated in spoken speech by the use of adjective or adverb modifiers, the connotation of a word may itself express intensity.

Examples:

I was *terrified*. (6a4)—This is a stronger word than "I was afraid" or "I felt worried."
I was *really* upset. (6a4)
I felt *terribly* ashamed. (5a4)
He felt *so* lonely. (3b3)
I was frightened *out of my wits*. (6a4)
The idea of having a tooth pulled *petrifies* me. (2a4)

5. A score assigned to a codable clause is also increased by one point if increased intensity is indicated by a series.

Examples:

She felt confused, tense, and frustrated. (6b3)
I was broken, bloody, and beaten. (2a4)
It was a scary, weird, and threatening experience. (6a4)
I had lost my mother, father, everything I loved. (3a4) and (1b2)

6. The *only* type of clause which is given more than one anxiety score is that which involves a statement regarding the death of animate others which is also verbalized as a loss to the self.

Example:

I lost both my parents in an accident last year. (1b2) and (3a3)

Note that "He lost both his parents in an accident last year" would be scored only for death anxiety (1b2), since the loss is verbalized to others and not the self.

7. Expressions of what may be called "bound" anxiety as opposed to "free" anxiety are *not* scored. Bound anxiety is rarely encountered in clearly recognizable form in verbal samples. Statements of the sort "The doctor said that there was nothing wrong, but I still couldn't move my arms," "I have a mental block," "I am obsessed with noses," "I feel compelled to work my hands all the time" would *not* be scored. If a clear expression of anxiety is present in the context, the clause is codable: "I was too scared to move a muscle" is scored (6a4).

8. Since the dynamics of denial of anxiety (or other affects) are extremely complex, we do not attempt to use a broad interpretation of the denial of anxiety or to utilize all the concepts of adaptation via this psychological mechanism. Rather, in the statements which we label "denial," we adhere to a rather simple and straightforward definition of denial.

Examples:

I was not afraid. (6d1)
It didn't cut me at all. (2d1)
I'm not a bit lonely. (3d1)
She's not afraid to die. (1d1)

9. We have followed a convention of scoring anxiety in blue—either blue pencil or blue pen. The use of distinctive colors for each of the scales aids in ready identification of what scale has been applied to a verbal sample and makes tabulation somewhat easier. Where the same copy of a verbal sample is scored for several different scales, the blue color differentiates the anxiety coding from other coding.

In the remainder of this section, each subcategory of the Anxiety Scale is briefly discussed and is followed by a fairly comprehensive list of examples of coded clauses. The numerous examples are included primarily as an aid to those persons who are learning the use of the scale or wish to utilize this manual as a practical adjunct in teaching technicians to score with the Anxiety Scale. Not only are there examples for the six major subcategories of the Anxiety Scale, but where a subcategory is itself variously defined, examples are included for the appropriate key words.

We wish to make it clear that we do not conceive of the separate words used in any of the subtypes of anxiety as discrete subcategories. Such words are intended rather to particularize and circumscribe the range of meaning which is intended for each of the major subtypes.

In all the examples which follow, the clauses are separated by diagonal marks. Clauses included for purposes of context, but not scored on this scale, are enclosed in parentheses.

The final pages of this section contain one-page excerpts of verbal samples, coded for anxiety. A brief tabulation, the total corrected score, and the square-root transformation are to be found on the pages following the verbal samples.

EXAMPLES OF ANXIETY

Death Anxiety (1)

Fear of death has been singled out by existentialists as the origin of all human anxiety (Kierkegaard, 1944; Tillich, 1944; Horney, 1945), but in our classification we have included only those items dealing directly with death and destruction. In general, references to death, dying, the threat of death (from external sources or internal situation), or anxiety about death are all considered as scorable in this category. References to the destruction of inanimate objects and a denial of death anxiety are also to be scored as death anxiety. The following specific rules are to be followed with regard to this category.

1. *All references to "war" are given a score 1b2* except in cases where the word "war" is used as an adjective; that is, "war bond" or "war canoe" is not scored.

2. References to *morgues, graveyards, tombstones, funeral homes, etc., are scored for death anxiety, usually 1b2.*

3. References to *suicide* of speaker or self-destruction or threats to kill the self are *not scored* as death anxiety unless specific reference is made to the suicide *idea* troubling or *making the self anxious.* Thus, such statements as "I wanted to kill myself," "I thought of turning on the gas," and "I tried to slash my wrists" are *not* coded. However, "I tried to get up courage to do away with myself" implies that the person is afraid to do so, and is

coded for death anxiety. References to suicide or threats of self-destruction by others are coded even if they are not embedded in a context of anxiety.

4. It is sometimes assumed that almost any reference to a *heart attack* or to having *cancer* is indicative of death anxiety. Unless the context in which such serious physical conditions are mentioned indicates *fear of death*, they are *not* in general *to be scored*. Naturally, if the subject makes such a clear-cut statement as "I thought that heart attack would be the end of me," death anxiety is clearly present and is scored. However, this kind of unambiguous statement will be found shading off into flat statements of "I had a heart attack," "She has cancer," etc., in which there is no clear-cut indication in either the clause per se or the general context in which the statement appears that the speaker is exhibiting anxiety or fear of death for himself or attributing it to others.

5. We have developed some rules for scoring clauses referring to "hunting" and "fishing." We have followed the convention of coding "hunting" for death anxiety, unless it is the self or self and others who are the subject. "He went hunting," for example, is scored as others causing death to animate others ($1b2$), while "I went hunting" would not be scored, since the self is the agent of destruction. However, references to "fishing" are *not* scored unless there is a clear statement about the fish being caught. For example, "He went fishing" is *not* scored, but "He caught a two-pound trout" is scored. Our thinking here has been that there is a qualitative difference in the motivation accompanying these two activities, and frequently references to fishing have appeared to be more involved with quiet contemplation than an active threat to the fish.

EXAMPLES OF DEATH ANXIETY (1)

References to death, dying, threat of death, or anxiety about death experienced by or occurring to:

Self (1a3)

(I thought) / I wouldn't come out of the shock treatment.
(I thought) / I was a goner.
(He was so mad) / he might have killed me.
My heart's going to give out.
He like to have killed all of us with his drunken driving.
My demise seemed to be rapidly approaching.

(If the house would catch on fire) / me and my little girl would have no way of getting out. (Code 1c1 for first clause and 1a3 for second.)
(They thought) / I wouldn't be able to make it back to shore.
(I dreamed) / I read of my funeral in the paper.
(They tell me) / I am lucky to pull through alive.
I almost drowned / (when I was a kid).
The bombs were falling all around us.
They sent me right into the front lines of the battle.
That car was coming straight at me.
They called the priest to give me last rites.
She seemed to be trying to strangle me.

Animate others (1b2)

She was sorry about the baby being born dead.
President Kennedy's wife, the late president, is moving to New York.
White Communist bullets were fired at them.
The Vietnam camp was attacked by the Reds.
I would be sent to the slaughter house for meat for lunch.
Billboards endanger the lives of motorists.
That was about the time my husband died.
Some people get killed or injured doing that.
A friend of mine just passed away.
He took his own life.
(If they get sprayed with gasoline), / they become a human torch.
It's very dangerous work, putting out oil fires.
They ran around like chickens / with their heads cut off.
Their plane was downed over Japan.
The report told about the fall of the Philippines.
Our plane went right over the cemetery there.
Some guys ran over a rabbit.
This is the anniversary of the bombing of Hiroshima.
He went to visit his brother's grave.
I was playing war with my roommate.
They were embalming the body.
I went to her funeral last year.
My husband was sent to Germany during the war.
When they passed away / (the house was sold).
The dog had been poisoned.
My dog could hunt down any opposum.
They caught a beauty of a large trout.
(As Tennyson said) / he "lay lingering out a five year's death in life."

Inanimate objects destroyed (1c1)

Those flowers are beginning to die.
They used dynamite to kill the oxygen / (that fed the fire).

(We stopped at this one farmhouse) / that was dead as a doornail.
The house was crushed by the airplane.
I like to listen to Broken Arrow on TV.
Fireworks plants frequently catch on fire.
The cable leading to the battery burned out.
The whole motorcycle was demolished.
The cup smashed into pieces.
The dog chewed the slipper into nothing.
The baby pulled the doll apart.
The building was wrecked by the explosion.
The carrier Lexington was sunk. (Note that there is no mention of animate others in this clause, and hence it is coded for destruction to an inanimate object. Unless the clause is in a context where people are threatened, the most objective interpretation calls for only the inanimate object type of coding.)

Denial of death anxiety (1d1)

Going to funerals doesn't bother me.
I'm not worrying about dying yet.
I really wasn't afraid of being hit by a bullet.
The idea of drowning has never bothered me.

Mutilation Anxiety (2)

Mutilation anxiety and fear, as we have conceptualized them, are synonymous with "castration" anxiety.

References to mutilation or castration anxiety are scored only when the injury, physical damage, etc., or the threat of such is *obvious* or *traumatic*. If the mutilation or injury is either obvious or traumatic, it is scorable whether the reference is to a small part of the body or to the entire body. References to pain, operations, hurts, or illnesses are not scored unless the context of the statement clearly indicates that anxiety or obvious and traumatic mutilation is also present.

EXAMPLES OF MUTILATION ANXIETY (2)

References to injury, tissue or physical damage, or anxiety about injury or threat of such experienced by or occurring to:

Self (2a3)

The outside of my skin is all off.
(While I was driving down the street) / someone ran into me.
Some of my teeth have already been yanked.
I worry about having to take shock treatments.

I got sunburned.
The machine mangled the fingers on my left hand.
I broke my leg doing it.
We were given first aid after the accident.
I got hit in the head with a baseball.
I can't walk now without a cane.
He broke my jawbone during scrimmage.
The test tube blew up right in my face.
They took all that blood out of my right arm.
She pulled my hair / (as hard as she could).
(I feel as though) / my womb is hanging out.
Now (because of the operation) I can't have babies.
It feels like / my insides are raw in there.
That medicine burns me.
They beat me with switches.

Animate others (2b2)

His cheek is going to be all puffed up.
Injuries and disability claims were recorded at the dispensary.
There are many accidents over weekends.
He had a fractured rib.
(She thought) / her plane was going to crash.
He has practically lost his eyesight.
The little cat had its paw crushed.
Her appendix was ruptured.
The cat bit the dog's ear.
(She was up all night) / because the dog's ear bled so.
I gave some money to the cripple on the corner.
(It looked like) / he might be dismembered.
It tore a gash in his knee.
They had to remove the tip of his thumb.
I went to the Marshall Islands for the atomic bomb test.

Inanimate objects (2c1)

The boat has a hole in it.
There was an oil-well explosion.
It was a weatherbeaten house on the seashore.
Bill broke the window.
The lining was all torn and frayed.
The flood water stood in all our houses.
He might have had a flat tire.
The piano was damaged in moving.
Lightning struck our neighbor's chimney.
The catfish broke his line.
That page got torn up / (before I had a chance to read it).
The vase was chipped.

The walls are flaking.
The zipper was beyond repair.
(I read) / where an airplane crashed into a house.
The car door was bent out of shape.
The wallpaper hung in rags.
There was a cigarette burn on the corner of the couch.
The cat tore the stuffing out of the chair.
We rummaged through the junk yard.
It was half burnt.

Denial of mutilation anxiety (2d1)

I don't think you will harm me.
The shot didn't hurt me at all.
I wasn't afraid of being stung.
I don't get nervous about operations.
I never worry about their hurting themselves.
None of the drivers seemed concerned about accidents.

Separation Anxiety (3)

The concept of separation anxiety and the descriptive items designating what references in speech are to be scored under this heading have been derived from psychoanalytic psychology. Freud (1936) postulated that in early infancy, up to about one and one-half years of age, the infant suffered separation anxiety through actual or threatened object loss. As the infant progressed from the oral incorporative through the oral aggressive and into the early anal stage, fear of loss of love of a significant other person replaced or was added to the simpler form of separation anxiety.

Bowlby (1960) and others have focused on the high importance of separation anxiety in personality formation, and this type of anxiety has been considered by many authorities to be of more primal significance and more disrupting to normal emotional development than what has been called "castration" or mutilation anxiety. Otto Rank's preoccupation with what he considered to be the catastrophic effects of birth trauma is, perhaps, an extreme example of separation anxiety. The baby's reflexive cry to a sudden, transient loss of physical support does suggest an instinctual separation anxiety. At older ages in the child's development, the fear of loss of a mother's love, feelings of a parental rejection, the fear of being sent up to one's room, and feelings of desertion and loneliness are all varieties of experiences highly associated with the construct of separation anxiety.

While the examples have been classified according to the various descriptive words used to delineate separation anxiety, there is much overlap; in some instances, a statement included as illustrative of one type of separation anxiety could as well be used to illustrate another.

EXAMPLES OF SEPARATION ANXIETY (3)

References to desertion, abandonment, ostracism, loss of support, loneliness, falling, loss of love or love object, or threat of such experienced by or occurring to:

Self (3a3)

DESERTION AND ABANDONMENT:

(Most of them had gone home), / but I couldn't go.
(I had been hurt) / and I was there all by myself.
My husband has left me.
We got lost on the way.
They didn't even come to see me.
My sister has not been writing to me lately.
(Maybe he will take me home / but I don't know), / if he will or not.
Don't my people want me?
Why did they have to forget me?
Why do they want to put me away?
(I ran out of gas) / and we were stranded there.
I was without a mother at the age of nine.
He never came back to me.

OSTRACISM:

He only talks to me through the children.
(I used to live there) / before they locked me up.
They don't like me very well.
He refused to be friends with me.
They don't want me around them.
My oldest son refuses to have anything to do with me.
No one would play with me but Elizabeth.
I have always felt a little rejected.
I'm not wanted here.
(Because I was a Negro) / I couldn't get a cup of coffee nowhere on the highway.
They put me out of the Air Force because of a bad stomach.
(I didn't know) / if the fraternity would cut me.
I would have felt really terrible about not being accepted for membership. (3a4)

FALLING:

(I thought) / I was going to fall flat on my face.
I almost fell off the curb.
We were thrown off the motorcycle.
I was afraid of going over the edge.
(I like to skate) / if I accidentally don't fall.

LOSS OF SUPPORT:

(It's surprising) / how hard it is / (after you leave the hosptital).
He had me put off welfare.
That bridge doesn't look strong enough to hold me.
I can't get within ten feet of the pond without slipping in the mud.
My wife won't back me up / (when I argue with them).
My huband was a poor provider.
(My mother and father's too old) / and they can't take me in.
They laid a bunch of us off during their slack periods.
(Sometimes he would pay the rent) / and sometimes he wouldn't.
I ain't got no dough any more.
I ain't got nobody to keep me up.

LOSS OF LOVE OR LOVE OBJECT:

(I wanted to talk to my mother) / but we were no longer very close.
I miss my family.
(I didn't want a divorce) / but he did.
I miss the girls // who give parties // so much. ($3a4$)
(He always has more friends) / than I do.
She wouldn't let me have my children after that.
My husband started going out with another girl.
(My husband had to go to Korea) / and I was heartbroken. ($3a4$)
We miss our regular nurse today.
$$3a3$$
(We was good pals) / but today we can't be / because of my being
$$3a3$$
   in hospital we can't be together.
I didn't get to go out.
I can't get off the ward any.
I took it very hard (father's death). ($3a4$ and $1b2$)
The doctor disapproved of my pass.
They stole my purse.

LONELINESS:

(It feels) / like I'm a thousand miles from home.
I'm lonelier now / (than I've ever been). ($3a4$)
They put me in solitary confinement.

I felt lonesome / (after they left).
I live in a solitary kind of way.
The house seemed too secluded to me.

Animate others (3b2)

DESERTION AND ABANDONMENT:

He left her with three small children to support.
She deserted her family to run off with him.
Her son refuses to live with her any more.
(He said) / he felt like a voice crying in the wilderness.
(He feels) / as if he had no one any more.
My dad left my mother / (when I was two).
He couldn't get out of the cave / (because his leg was caught).
They were going to dump the dog out there.

OSTRACISM:

Nobody ever asks for her phone number.
They made her ride in the Negro section of the train.
They told him to leave town and not come back.
Those men were rejected for various reasons.
They blackballed that candidate.
(He told me) / he was through with her.
The Protestant missionaries tried to keep the Catholic priest out of the islands.
(There was a little boy / that wanted to come in) / and they wouldn't let him come in.
My son was sent away.

LOSS OF SUPPORT:

The rope on the swing almost gave out with those heavy children.
She has nothing today.
(If he gets a better job) / they might cut down / what he's getting on welfare.
He will have nothing to fall back on in life.
There was so much unemployment then.
He never did support them any.
She slid right down the bank and into the river.
Some people can snap their fingers and cause others to lose their jobs.
The edge of the cliff started to crumble under his feet.
The wind took his raft out to the middle of the lake / (and he didn't know what to do).
The mother accidentally dropped her.
The ice was too thin for so many skaters.
No one would come to her aid in the debate.
He lost his anchor on that fishing trip.

FALLING:

He fell out of the tree.
Into the water she tumbled.
My buddy went head over heels down the steps.
The baby mouse fell off the table.

LOSS OF LOVE OR LOVE OBJECT:

(He told her) / he loved someone else.
He can't seem to keep any friends.
My parents are separated.
She *keenly felt* no longer being surrounded by the warmth of her family. (3b3)
Their car was stolen.
She was robbed on the way home.
The adoption agency will not let her have the child back.
There has been a lot of talk about stealing.
He was afraid of pickpockets.
She misses the other children.
She couldn't find her mother in the crowd.
The other patients have lost their privileges.
(Mr. Deeds was angry) / that their passes were turned down.
They started a search party for him.

LONELINESSS

She was a lonely child.
He was a lone wolf.
(I hope) / the lonesomeness doesn't get him down.

Inanimate objects (3c1)

The tail pipe fell off the car.
The lonely wood was very dark.
The flower pot dropped off the window sill.
The poem was about a lonely isle.
The tractor slipped from the road and into the ditch.
It was a desolate house.

Denial of separation anxiety (3d1)

    3d1   3a3
I don't mind / (that they wouldn't talk to me).
             3d1   3b2
(He said) / he didn't care / (if he did lose friends because of joining a fraternity).
She wasn't afraid to be left alone out there.
I never worry about going home by myself.
I've never been concerned about falling from a roof.

Guilt Anxiety (4)

In our descriptive items differentiating between shame and guilt anxiety, we have leaned on the work of Piers and Singer (1953).

As stated in the discussion of the Anxiety-Fear Scale (p. 16), no attempt is made to distinguish between whether the stimulus to the affect which we have labeled guilt anxiety has an internal or an external genesis. Obviously, there is a vast difference between such statements as "I'm afraid I'm a bad citizen" and "The police found out about the car I stole." We do not distinguish, however, between content in which the speaker does, in fact, criticize and condemn the self, thus connoting guilt, and one which describes a situation in which the speaker is being criticized by others or threatened with such criticism. The rationale for including statements in which the speaker recounts actions or situations in which criticism, disapproval, or condemnation have been or might be expressed by others is that such statements can imply both the subject's projection of his internalized or introjected feelings to a situation outside himself and also some of the dynamics of what Freud called "the unconscious need for punishment." While we do not confound "feelings of guilt" with apprehension about being "caught" or impending punishment, we do not attempt to discriminate between them.

The use of the phrase "getting into trouble" is extremely common in the verbal samples of such groups as juvenile delinquents, incarcerated criminals, and those from lower socioeconomic groups. This colloquialism appears to be a euphemistic way of revealing that one has been criticized or threatened with criticism by those in authority: teachers, school principals, police, guards, etc. Many statements of this nature are therefore coded for guilt anxiety.[2]

EXAMPLES OF GUILT ANXIETY (4)

References to adverse criticism, abuse, condemnation, moral disapproval, guilt, or threat of such experienced by:

---

[2] For an excellent discussion of lower class use of and concern with "getting into trouble," see Walter B. Miller, "Lower Class Culture as a Generating Milieu of Gang Delinquency," in *The Sociology of Crime and Delinquency*, ed. M. E. Wolfgang, L. Savity, and N. Johnson (New York: Wiley and Sons, 1962).

Self (4a3)

ADVERSE CRITICISM:

(My parents didn't approve) / of what I did.
(Are you trying to tell me) / I don't behave?
They accused us of it.
I got in trouble again with that teacher.
(They said) / I neglected my daughter.
They don't think / (I'm sane).
He scolded me for not losing weight.
(He says) / I'm too lazy to work.
The things // I say // might be wrong.
(I realize) / I was being unfair.
My girl friend got mad at me.
My husband was angry / (because I wanted to work).
(I told you) / I wasn't a very good patient.
She's looking for me for nonsupport.
(The audience knows) / if you make a mistake.
I'm never ready on time.

ABUSE:

She would scream and swear at me.
I'm insulted by all this.
The nurses aren't treating me right.
They run all over me on the ward.
(I'm treated) / like I was a nigger or something.
We got these threatening letters from them.
They grabbed me and questioned me.
The doctor even was sarcastic to me.
At the reform school I got only cruelty.

CONDEMNATION:

I felt terrible about the lies / (they told about me). (4a4)
I get so bad / (I can't even give my family a good word). (4a4)
My piano teacher was really disgusted with my playing.
I was cited for running a red light.
As a kid I was always doomed to punishment.
I went to jail.
They thought / I was a spy.
The cops were chasing us.
They found out / (about the car I stole).
They put me on probation.
His family thought / I was unfit.
I came in to court for auto larceny.
We confessed.

(He told them) / my conduct was disgraceful.
I had to go before the judge to hear my sentence.

MORAL DISAPPROVAL:

(I know) / I have been unjust to her.
They always tell on me.
I drink too much.
That's all my fault.
We got into trouble for smoking behind the barn.
It was reprehensible on my part.
I had violated one of the laws / (that I live by).
It's time for me to grow up and start being less selfish.
(He thought) / I was wrong to like dancing.
The devil won't stand for us to live in sin.

GUILT:

(I didn't listen to my mother) / like I should have.
I had guilty feelings about having relations with a married man.
I was blamed for it.
Just thinking // (of how I neglected the children) // made me feel really terrible. (4a4)
She always has a look of reproof / (when she looks at me).
(I kept feeling) / that I was wrong to want such things.
(If I have made mistakes) / I am sorry for them.
It is awful to live with a conscience like mine.
(I don't want her to pay for it) / so she won't have no comeback on me.
There I learned the burden of hate.

Animate others (4b2)

ADVERSE CRITICISM:

The majority of the people of our country oppose the atheism of the Soviet government.
The article said / it was the fault of the poor.
My mother would scold the cat.
They say / Lee Oswald was an awful troublemaker.
The orderly called her a stupid jerk.
The people in urban redevelopment don't appear very successful to the voters / (who are impatient).
She fusses at him pretty much.
He got demerits for it.
There was a lot of racial prejudice. (Note that there is no specific reference to ostracism; see separation anxiety, ostracism, pp. 40 ff.)
(Some people say) / he's bad-tempered.

She couldn't stand him.
(He was told) / he had absolutely no ear for music.
My mother had no use / (for the man I married).
My parents were always criticizing each other.
The family felt / she was a disgrace to them.

ABUSE:

(He felt) / they had no right to treat him so badly.
He was always hollering and cursing at my mother.
The attendants were sometimes cruel.
They were horribly mean to him. (4b3)
Their treatment of the prisoners was inhumane.

CONDEMNATION:

The dog was put out for being bad.
He had to go to court for a hearing.
The committee voted to censure him.
He could have been fired for picking up passengers.
(The other students thought) / he was beyond contempt.
The police finally caught him.
The prisoners were in the yard.
They caught some men trying to sell wine to the patients.

MORAL DISAPPROVAL:

The police already had a record of the misdeeds of those children.
(His family thought) / he was spending too much time away from home with the wrong people.
(They thought) / the kids' liking for rock and roll was pretty bad.
They were scared of being found there.
(They knew) / as minors they shouldn't buy liquor.
He had the reputation of being a reprobate.
(No matter what he did / he always thought) / he was wrong.
He felt guilty.
(She knows) / she is sinning.
(Inside himself he knew) / he should have given them a better price for their car.

Denial of guilt anxiety (4d1)

He protested his innocence.
I asked for a lie detector test.
(I hope / she understood) / that I would have been there / (if I could). (At mother's deathbed.)
(I always did / as I should have) / at least I was never in trouble before.
That's not my fault.
She shouldn't blame me for it.
I'm not a sinner.

Shame Anxiety (5)

Although we have followed the thinking of Piers and Singer (1953) in differentiating shame from guilt, we have not for purposes of our scale development attempted to distinguish between what Piers defines as "the structure of shame" and the concept of "inferiority feelings." In the latter type of affect, one may be less concerned with the struggle between ego and ego-ideal and more directly involved with comparisons between external criteria, comparison with others, etc. Hence, although we recognize the conceptual differences between these two ideas, we do not believe it possible to differentiate between them using content analysis alone. Consistent with this rather broad definition of shame, we include all references to ridicule, inadequacy, shame, embarrassment, etc. and do not attempt to discriminate between whether the stimulus to this affect is internalized or externalized.

EXAMPLES OF SHAME ANXIETY (5)

References to ridicule, inadequacy, shame, embarrassment, humiliation, overexposure of deficiencies or private details, or threat of such experienced by:

Self (5a3)

RIDICULE:

Why should I sit here like a kid?
They make fun of me.
He twitted me about being fat.
I really feel utterly ridiculous in a situation like that. (5a4)
He can't just go on and on mocking me.
I was aware of my own triteness.
The eyes seemed to taunt me.
They just stared at me and laughed.
(It was one of those deriding remarks) / that he makes to me.
I'm being silly.
They make disparaging remarks / (when they think / I don't know it).
What do you take me for, a stump?

INADEQUACY:

You have me sweating here for something to say.
I've lost my habits / (and I have to gain them back gradually).
(I want to help myself) / but I don't know how to do it.
Where was I / when brains were passed out?

We didn't get enough education.
I'm lacking in education.
Everybody is always ahead of me.
(I liked sewing class) / but I didn't make such good grades.
I never do as well / (as I think / I should).
I'm stumped for something to say.
I'm lost for words.
I'm like a little girl.
I don't ever have anything interesting to talk about.
My vocabulary is very limited.
I never knew how to take care of my son.
I don't know what to say. (But do *not* code if this is modified, as in "I don't know what *else* to say.")
I feel stupid sitting here like this.
My mind is a complete blank.

SHAME AND EMBARRASSMENT:

I was so ashamed / (of how our home looked). (5a4)
I feel funny with her / (because she's young).
I felt myself blushing.
(He told me) / I had behaved improperly.
(I guess) / that's a shortcoming of mine.
I talk too loud.
I must have turned about fifteen different colors.
(You can imagine) / how I felt about having to go on welfare.
(This is so sudden) / I feel confused.
It's disconcerting to sit here and say nothing.
I've always been extremely self-conscious. (5a4)
It was degrading to have to ring the doorbell to get in every night.
I can only think of nonsense to talk about.
I was shy as a child.
(I guess) / I did look disreputable.
It's embarrassing to me to go into a room of strangers.
He tries to discredit me in the children's eyes.
It still hits a chord / when people call me skinny.
I felt so unworthy of him. (5a4)

HUMILIATION:

(I don't know) / what was wrong with me to let myself go like that.
It was a very humbling experience.
It's degrading to have to do things like that.
I had very little self-respect left.

OVEREXPOSURE OF DEFICIENCIES OR PRIVATE DETAILS:

I have to sit here and say nothing.
I don't even know how to wipe my ass.

Perhaps I'm not revealing enough about myself.
I'm too self-conscious to talk about anything.
I didn't want to talk about such personal things.
They shouldn't watch me irrigate my colostomy.

Animate others (5b2)

RIDICULE:

They joked about him / (because he couldn't add).
He got a lot of razzing over that incident.
He doesn't want to be called chicken.
He was the butt of all their jokes.
(She felt) / they were being disparaging.
The other kids kept taunting him.
His parents twitted him about his girl friend.
(They somehow got the impression) / they were being mocked.

INADEQUACY:

He felt other people looked down on him.
It's hard for him / (because his brother is so smart).
(She knows) / she was disappointing her family.
(He felt) / he was a failure.
(My sister feels) / she can't begin to keep up with her friends.

SHAME AND EMBARRASSMENT:

He was really ashamed about having to go to the principal's office. (5b3)
His mother shamed him into going.
It made God ashamed of Himself to make orange trees.
She blushed and turned red and everything.
Under those circumstances anyone would feel abashed.
He had a kind of self-conscious laugh.
Her embarrassment was obvious to everyone.
He always was pretty shy with them.
She had a lot of feeling about being fat. (5b3)

HUMILIATION:

They hated to get beaten by such a poor team.
He felt real dumb / when the other kids laughed about it.
The teacher really sort of held them up as objects of scorn.
They shouldn't have the right to humiliate the pledges that way.

OVEREXPOSURE OF DEFICIENCIES OR PRIVATE DETAILS:

He didn't like to take his clothes off in front of the doctor.
He tried his best to hide / (how his family had treated him).

He attempted to keep the rip in his pants from showing by walking sideways.
He was afraid / (he might not make a good impression).

Denial of shame anxiety (5d1)

I'm not ashamed to admit it.
I've stopped worrying about not being as smart as others.
They never treat us like patients. (Speaker is a patient.)
I don't really care / (if they do kid about me).
Their jokes don't bother me any.
I don't feel / I've been a failure in life.

Diffuse or Nonspecific Anxiety (6)

Often in the content analysis of small samples of speech, it is impossible to distinguish the type of anxiety-fear which is being expressed, although it is clear that it is present. Attached to the Anxiety Scale is a list of words which serve as guides or indicators in interpreting expressions which may be scored in this subcategory. It should be clear, however, that the use of these words does not in itself denote diffuse anxiety if the context of the clause is indicative of an affect which may properly be scored in one of the first five subcategories. For instance, a statement reading "I was *timid* about entering a room full of unknown people" would be coded for shame anxiety rather than in the diffuse or nonspecific category. Or, "I was timid about walking so close to the edge of the cliff" would be scored in the separation anxiety subcategory. Only when one cannot clearly and unambiguously determine the source or type of anxiety-fear is the clause coded in the diffuse or nonspecific subcategory.

There are several frequently used words that may or may not be scorable, depending on their context. "Trouble" as indicative of diffuse anxiety is distinguished from the use of "getting into trouble" (which is scored for guilt anxiety) or the connotation of "trouble" as synonymous with annoyance or difficulty. For example, the clause "The trouble with the car was minor" connotes "the difficulty with the car," or "The weather is likely to give us trouble" is indicative of annoyance. The coding of "trouble" for diffuse anxiety should involve the idea of worry, anxiety, being perturbed, or being disturbed.

"Uncomfortable" is another word leading to problems in scoring. It sometimes has the meaning of *uneasy,* which is codable as diffuse or nonspecific anxiety (6a3) unless the context dictates one of the other subcategories. However, it may be used to indicate physical feelings of pain, discomfort, unpleasantness, or distress and in such a context is not scorable.

A third word that is difficult to score is "bother," which sometimes means perplexity or annoyance (not scored) and at other times is used to indicate a source of worry or a quality of being troubled. Again, the context is very important in the decision to code or not.

Clauses may also be coded in this category if it is impossible to distinguish between two categories, that is, between mutilation and separation anxiety in such a statement as "We were rather leary about going out on the ice." One also uses the diffuse subcategory if a pronoun such as "it" or "that" is so far from the original reference that one can no longer be sure of the specific meaning, although the context is clearly codable for anxiety.

EXAMPLES OF DIFFUSE OR NONSPECIFIC ANXIETY (6)

References by word (see pp. 60–61) or in phrases to anxiety and/or fear without distinguishing type or source of anxiety:

Self (6a3)

It seems like / I'm scared of something all the time.
(There isn't anything / the doctors can do) / when I'm upset.
That medicine doesn't seem to calm me down.
That always worried me.
(People say, / "Don't let it worry you,") / but I can't help it. (6d1 and 6a3)
All // I have now // is this one big fear. (6a4)
My kids get on my nerves / (when they play in the house)
She had me frightened.
I only get upset / (when something like that happens).
I was a complete bundle of nerves. (6a4)
I worried a lot over that job. (6a4)
Some of the problems facing me are frightening.
Most of my concern is for her and the children.

Animate others (6b2)

Being cooped up in the house kept her nervous.
She was always concerned about her children.
Most of the boys are a little edgy just now.
My mother was in a real state. (6b3)
She had qualms about going.

She's worrying now about her graduation.
She became panicky and shook up. (6b3)
He seemed ready to crack up altogether.
He dreaded for five o'clock to come.
She was apprehensive about it.

Denial (6d1)

That doesn't bother me any more.
I didn't worry about that.
It didn't seem to make me nervous at all.
Some people aren't troubled by these things.
She wasn't tense at all.
(I don't agree with you) / that I'm nervous.

Next are included six verbal samples coded for anxiety, each followed by the correct tabulation for the subcategories and the square-root transformation yielding a corrected total score. The first verbal sample is rather clear and unambiguous. Succeeding ones have been included because the problems involved in coding required greater discrimination in the use of the scales.

Verbal Sample # 1 Coded for Anxiety

Name of Subject:
   (Male psychiatric inpatient)   Interviewer:
Date: Total Words: 187
Name of Study: Correction Factor: 0.5348

                            5a3
What do you want me to say? / I don't know what to talk about. /
                  5a3
Well, let's see . . . / I don't know what to talk about, Doc. / Uh I've been here for about four months / and uh had a pretty rough time of it. / And and uh my wife, she wants me to stay here / as long as
                        6a3
I can. / I I told her / I would. / Our babies, they get on my nerves, my little babies. / Sometimes I don't get no sleep. / (Pause) Got a
               2b2   2b2
little cat at home. / It got hurt, / it got a broken leg / and I had to get that fixed. / (Pause) I had a pretty rough time of it. / My dad,
1b2   3a3
I lost my dad in '54, / now only got two brothers living. / And they
      3a3   4a3
never come to see me. / I guess / it's pretty much my fault. / And uh my wife she she changes her mind all the time. / I think / she's
     6b2   4b2
kind of nervous too. / She thinks / she hears people saying bad things

          6a4
about her. / I get sort of frightened and scared about it all. / I don't know / what else I can tell you. / That's all / I can think of. /

TABULATION OF VERBAL SAMPLE # 1 CODED FOR ANXIETY
Correction Factor (C.F.) = 0.5348

Subcategory	Total weight (W.)	Raw score (W. × C.F.)
Death		
1b2 × 1	2	1.07
Mutilation		
2b2 × 2	4	2.14
Separation		
3a3 × 2	6	3.21
Guilt		
4a3 × 1		
4b2 × 1	5	2.67
Shame		
5a3 × 2	6	3.21
Diffuse		
6a4 × 1		
6a3 × 1	9	4.81
6b2 × 1		
Total	32	17.11

17.11 + ½ C.F. = 17.38
Square root = 4.17

Verbal Sample # 2 Coded for Anxiety

Name of Subject:
 (Male medical inpatient)   Interviewer:
Date: Total Words: 188
Name of Study: Correction Factor: 0.5319

             5a3
Well, here I am again doing this. / If I knew something to talk about / I could / I could / I could tell it better. / I don't know / whether this goes over to the Board of Directors or what / but I do /
          5a3
the best I know for a poor uneducated old man. / Everything I know
      5a3   4a3
about myself / I like to keep to myself. / Well, maybe the law is try-
           4d1
ing to find out about me. / I was never arrested before in my life. /
  4a3   4a3
I'd like to get arrested sometimes / just to see how it feels to go to
      5a3   5a3
jail. / I guess / I sound / like I'm off my rocker. / But what little I
     5a3
know, / why it ain't hardly worth the telling. / That nurse, she came to get more blood this afternoon. / I just held out my arm / she

                    2a3   2a3
jabbed me with a needle. / Seems like / I'll run out of blood. / I
          2a3   2a3
won't have any left. / Been jabbed so much now, / I got a black and
          2a3   4a3
blue spot in my arm. / I don't know / what'll happen to me / after
                                3a3
I make these complaints. / So they might discharge me / even if I
am sick. /

TABULATION OF VERBAL SAMPLE # 2 CODED FOR ANXIETY
Correction Factor (C.F.) = 0.5319

Subcategory	Total weight	Raw score
Death	0	....
Mutilation		
2a3 × 5	15	7.98
Separation		
3a3 × 1	3	1.60
Guilt		
4a3 × 4	13	6.91
4d1 × 1		
Shame		
5a3 × 6	18	9.57
Diffuse	0	....
Total	49	26.06

26.06 + ½ C.F. = 26.33
Square root = 5.13

Verbal Sample # 3 Coded for Anxiety

Name of Subject:
  (Female medical inpatient)   Interviewer:
Date: Total Words: 192
Name of Study: Correction Factor: 0.5208

I worked up at that plant for 23 years / and I liked it pretty much. /
                              4a3
And a lot of girls was jealous of me working, putting out so much
                              4a3
work / and they made it pretty bad for me at times. / But I stuck
              5a3
there anyway. / I don't know what to say. / Well, I got caught in one
                    2a3   2a3
of the machines out there and got hurt. / My finger was mashed up
sort of. / But I was only off from work for about two days then. /
                                                3a3
And then when the plant closed / everybody had to leave, put out. /

                    3a3   6a4
And that kind of upset me too for a while. / I was really pretty afraid / when I first come in for these treatments / but then I found /
            6d1   6d1
it didn't bother me none at all. / So I've got over that, over that fear
                        6d1
now. / I can take them every time with no fear. / And I wish / my son would come up soon. / I been here three weeks now / and he
                3a3   4b2
still ain't been out to see me. / He got into trouble with the law last
                    6a3
year / and I worry some about him. / Is the five minutes over yet? /

TABULATION OF VERBAL SAMPLE # 3 CODED FOR ANXIETY
Correction Factor (C.F.) = 0.5208

Subcategory	Total weight	Raw score
Death	0	....
Mutilation		
2a3 × 2	6	3.12
Separation		
3a3 × 3	9	4.69
Guilt		
4a3 × 2		
4b2 × 1	8	4.17
Shame		
5a3 × 1	3	1.56
Diffuse		
6a4 × 1		
6a3 × 1	10	5.21
6d1 × 3		
Total	36	18.75

18.75 + ½ C.F. = 19.01
Square root = 4.36

Verbal Sample # 4 Coded for Anxiety

Name of Subject:
   (Female psychiatric outpatient)
Date:
Name of Study:

Interviewer:
Total Words: 209
Correction Factor: 0.4785

Ok, I guess / I'll tell you about my cat. / She is a rather small black
                                2b2
cat, but a rather vicious cat to other people. / She's had 18 litters of kittens in the last seven years. / One of her babies // that we kept // was very friendly and gentle. / She always protected him / even when
        2b2   1b2
he bit her tail / when he was playing. / But then he was killed out in

front of the house. / We always thought / that he would be / because he ran across the busy street frequently. / Let's see. / Back
to the mother, I guess. / Sometimes we'd find her sitting on the
$1b2$

$3b2$

roof. / Then she'd pretend / she couldn't get down, / and we'd always
$6b2$

climb up for her on a ladder. / One neighbor was afraid of our older
cat, / and then another was allergic to them. / So my mother used
$3b2$

to lock them out of the house / when that neighbor came to visit. /
Once we had a visitor along with her baby / and we could see / that
$3c1$

the baby was going to drop the ashtray / she was playing with. /
And the mother cat went over, stood up on the table with her front
$2b2$

feet / and she just smacked the baby's hands. / I had to laugh out
loud at that one. /

TABULATION OF VERBAL SAMPLE # 4 CODED FOR ANXIETY
Correction Factor (C.F.) = 0.4785

Subcategory	Total weight	Raw score
Death		
$1b2 \times 2$	4	1.91
Mutilation		
$2b2 \times 3$	6	2.87
Separation		
$3b2 \times 2$		
$3c1 \times 1$	5	2.39
Guilt		
	0	....
Shame		
	0	....
Diffuse		
$6b2 \times 1$	2	0.96
Total	17	8.13

8.13 + ½ C.F. = 8.37
Square root = 2.89

Verbal Sample # 5 Coded for Anxiety

Name of Subject: (Medical student)   Interviewer:
Date: Total Words: 175
Name of Study: Correction Factor: 0.5714

Well, let's see. / Traveling nearly 4,000 miles in an airplane for the
first time and stopping in various countries provided me with inter-
$6a3$

esting experiences with people. / A somewhat frightening experience

$2c1$

was / when one of the plane engines was found to be defective. / And we learned / just after we were out over the open sea / that it
$1a3$ $6b3$
had only been corrected temporarily. / Some of the passengers were
$6d1$
really frightened / but others acted / as if they didn't have a worry in the world. / However, these experiences were of necessity brief, and somewhat superficial but quite colorful and enlightening. / I'll have to think of something else now. / A rather interesting experience was / when a group of us used to spar in the gym. / Joe use to
$2b2$
get the worst of it. / As a matter of fact, whenever he hit someone
$2b2$ $2b2$
hard / he suffered the most / for he was always smashing up his
$3b2$
hands. / Another time, we were playing golf with Joe / and he fell
$2b2$
down / and badly skinned up his arms. / We really kidded him about it. /

TABULATION OF VERBAL SAMPLE # 5 CODED FOR ANXIETY
Correction Factor (C.F.) = 0.5714

	Subcategory	Total weight	Raw score
Death			
	$1a3 \times 1$	3	1.71
Mutilation			
	$2b2 \times 4$		
	$2c1 \times 1$	9	5.14
Separation			
	$3b2 \times 1$	2	1.14
Guilt		0	....
Shame		0	....
Diffuse			
	$6a3 \times 1$		
	$6b3 \times 1$	7	4.00
	$6d1 \times 1$		
Total		21	11.99

11.99 + ½ C.F. = 12.28
Square root = 3.50

Verbal Sample # 6 Coded for Anxiety

Name of Subject:
    (Male college student)   Interviewer:
Date: Total Words: 153
Name of Study: Correction Factor: 0.6536

Many interesting experiences // that I have had // probably do not
approach that of my auto accident. / It is true / that this is not a
    2a3
very pleasant experience / but you do sort of gain some insight into
                                                                2a3
many new thought processes. / Luckily for me, I was not very badly
hurt / and I only had to spend one week in the hospital. / The inter-
                                                    2a3
esting part about it was / when I awoke from being knocked uncon-
                                  1b2
scious / I had a very close feeling to my deceased father. / My dad
       1b2   2a3
had passed away several weeks / before I had the accident / and I
                                3a4
had been very lonely without him. / For a brief moment there when
                            1a3   3d1
I came to / I felt / that I was in heaven / and he was near to me. /
                                                          2a3
But then people rushed up / and they started asking / if I was hurt
                       3a3
badly / and the brief feeling of contact with my father was over and
done with. /

TABULATION OF VERBAL SAMPLE # 6 CODED FOR ANXIETY
Correction Factor (C.F.) = 0.6536

Subcategory	Total weight	Raw score
Death		
1a3 × 1		
1b2 × 2	7	4.58
Mutilation		
2a3 × 6	18	11.76
Separation		
3a4 × 1		
3a3 × 1		
3d1 × 1	8	5.23
Guilt	0	....
Shame	0	....
Diffuse	0	....
Total	33	21.57

21.57 + ½ C.F. = 21.90
Square root = 4.68

DIFFUSE ANXIETY

The following is a list of words of the kind that may be scored in category 6 if the type of anxiety is not explicitly stated or in any one of the other categories if the stimulus or source of the reaction is denoted. Any grammatical form of the word may be scored, whether it is an adjective, noun, adverb, or verb and so forth. The list is not intended to be complete but is provided mainly to give examples of scorable word concepts.

ADJECTIVES	NOUNS	ADVERBS	VERBS
agitated	agitation	agitatedly	to agitate
anxious	anxiety	anxiously	....
apprehensive	apprehension	....	....
....	concern	....	....
creepy	creepiness	creepily	....
dangerous	danger	dangerously	to endanger
desperate	desperation	desperately	to despair
disturbed	....	....	....
dreadful	dread	dreadfully	to dread
eerie	eeriness	eerily	....
fearful	fear	fearfully	to fear
frightened	fright	frightfully	to frighten
....	forboding	....	....
frustrated	frustration	frustratedly	to frustrate
irritable	irritation	irritably	to irritate
jittery	jitters	....	....
nervous	nerves	nervously	....
overwhelmed	....	overwhelmingly	to overwhelm
panicky	panic	....	to panic
rattled	....	....	to rattle
scared	....	scarily	to scare
shaky	....	shakily	to shake
tense	tension	tensely	to tense
terrified	terror	....	to terrorize
threatened	threat	threateningly	to threaten
timid	timidity	timidly	....
trembling	tremble	trembly	to tremble
troubled	trouble	....	to trouble
uncanny	....	uncannily	....
uneasy	uneasiness	uneasily	....
upset	upset	....	to upset
weird	weirdness	weirdly	....
worried	worry	worriedly	to worry

CHAPTER VII
The Hostility Directed Outward Scale

INTRODUCTION

The scoring categories of the Hostility Directed Outward Scale are ranged on a continuum that varies from a denial of hostility, through references to anger without an object, to hostility toward a situation or infrahuman objects, and finally to varying degrees of hostility toward human beings. The latter subcategories range from expressions of mild dislike or criticism of an individual to stronger expressions of verbal aggression and physical violence.

In addition to the intensity continuum, ranging in weights from one to three, the scale includes levels of awareness of hostility. Statements that refer to the aggressive or hostile feelings as having emanated from the speaker are classified as "overt" hostility directed outward. Aggression or hostility attributed to others as either active agents or passive recipients, and the denial of hostile feelings, are classified as "covert." Statements in which the speaker alone is the recipient of the aggressive act are not scored on this scale (see our Hostility Directed Inward and Ambivalently Directed Hostility Scales).

As noted above, the categories of both the overt and covert subscales of the Hostility Directed Outward Scale have been assigned weights according to the presumed intensity of the hostility implied by the statement. It should be noted, however, that unlike the Anxiety Scale (where if the affect is attributed, projected, or displaced to others, the weight is correspondingly lowered), on the Hostility Outward Scale the same weight is assigned to a specified subcategory (or degree of intensity) regardless of whether the speaker is the agent or attributes the hostile act or feeling to another.

A number of studies have been directed toward establishing the construct validity of this measure. Correlations have been obtained in different samples with clinical ratings of hostility using the Oken Scale (1960), such self-report measures as an adjective checklist, the Buss Hostility Inventory (1961), selected scores from the Mental Status Schedule (Spitzer, 1965; Spitzer *et al.*, 1967), and subscales derived from the Wittenborn Psychiatric Rating Scales (1955); correlations have also been obtained with some biochemical and physiological measures. In general, both the overt and covert scores on the verbal samples correlated positively with other measures of immediate hostility, such as the Oken rating and the adjective checklist. There is some evidence that the overt scale correlates with the paranoid scale of the MMPI and, to a lesser degree, with some of the subscales of the Buss Inventory and special subscales derived from the Wittenborn scales. In several samples of people studied, we have found higher correlations for males than for females, although there is no consistent difference in their average verbal hostility outward scores. For more details regarding the assumptions underlying this scale and normative data, reliability, and validity studies, the reader is referred to the companion publication (Gottschalk and Gleser, 1969).

The following pages of this section are devoted to:

1. *The Hostility Directed Outward Scale* (Schedule 2). The overt portion of the scale is labeled with a Roman numeral I and the covert portion with a Roman numeral II. The arabic numerals indicate the weight to be given to a specific subcategory, and the lower-case letters delineate various subcategories given equal weight.

2. *Rules for scoring hostility outward.* The scale is followed by the specific rules used for the scoring of verbal samples using this measure of aggression (see also the previous section on general rules applicable to all the Gottschalk-Gleser scales, p. 13).

3. *Examples of hostility outward.* Following the rules there is a list of examples for each subcategory of the scale. As in the section on the Anxiety Scale, the convention has been followed of enclosing in parentheses those clauses included for purposes of context. Additional demarcation of clauses, where necessary, have been indicated by diagonal marks.

The overt portion of the scale is presented first, followed by the covert subscale. In an attempt to be as exhaustive as possible, the examples are presented both in terms of the major subcategories of the scale and for the varying criteria within each subcategory. It is recognized that such detailed analysis leads to some overlapping and usage of definitions which are not discrete or which blend imperceptibly into one another. It is hoped, however, that the practical advantages of being provided with many illustrations of our scoring procedures will outweigh any disadvantages in this approach. Thus, it will be found that under I*b*1—self adversely criticizing, depreciating, blaming, or expressing anger or dislike of subhumans, inanimate objects, places, or situations—we present examples for the individual words in this subcategory although in some of their usages these words may be synonymous.

4. *Coded verbal samples.* The section ends with several one-page excerpts of verbal samples broken into the component clauses and coded for hostility directed outward. A tabulation of the scoring of each verbal sample is also given.

SCHEDULE 2

Hostility Directed Outward Scale: Destructive, Injurious, Critical Thoughts and Actions Directed to Others

I Hostility Outward—Overt

Thematic Categories

a 3* Self killing, fighting, injuring other individuals or threatening to do so.

b 3 Self robbing or abandoning other individuals, causing suffering or anguish to others, or threatening to do so.

c 3 Self adversely criticizing, depreciating, blaming, expressing anger, dislike of other human beings.

a 2 Self killing, injuring or destroying domestic animals, pets, or threatening to do so.

b 2 Self abandoning, robbing, domestic animals, pets, or threatening to do so.

c 2 Self criticizing or depreciating others in a vague or mild manner.

d 2 Self depriving or disappointing other human beings.

II Hostility Outward—Covert

Thematic Categories

a 3* Others (human) killing, fighting, injuring other individuals or threatening to do so.

b 3 Others (human) robbing, abandoning, causing suffering or anguish to other individuals, or threatening to do so.

c 3 Others adversely criticizing, depreciating, blaming, expressing anger, dislike of other human beings.

a 2 Others (human) killing, injuring, or destroying domestic animals, pets, or threatening to do so.

b 2 Others (human) abandoning, robbing, domestic animals, pets, or threatening to do so.

c 2 Others (human) criticizing or depreciating other individuals in a vague or mild manner.

d 2 Others (human) depriving or disappointing other human beings.

Schedule 2 (*contd.*)

I Hostility Outward—Overt	II Hostility Outward—Covert
Thematic Categories	Thematic Categories
	e 2 Others (human or domestic animals) dying or killed violently in death-dealing situation or threatened with such.
	f 2 Bodies (human or domestic animals) mutilated, depreciated, defiled.
a 1 Self killing, injuring, destroying, robbing wild life, flora, inanimate objects or threatening to do so.	*a* 1 Wild life, flora, inanimate objects, injured, broken, robbed, destroyed or threatened with such (with or without mention of agent).
b 1 Self adversely criticizing, depreciating, blaming, expressing anger or dislike of subhumans, inanimate objects, places, situations.	*b* 1 Others (human) adversely criticizing, depreciating, expressing anger or dislike of subhumans, inanimate objects, places, situations.
c 1 Self using hostile words, cursing, mention of anger or rage without referent.	*c* 1 Others angry, cursing without reference to cause or direction of anger. *Also* instruments of destruction not used threateningly.
	d 1 Others (human, domestic animals) injured, robbed, dead, abandoned or threatened with such from any source including subhuman and inanimate objects, situations (storms, floods, etc.).
	e 1 Subhumans killing, fighting, injuring, robbing, destroying each other or threatening to do so.
	f 1 Denial of anger, dislike, hatred, cruelty, and intent to harm.

* The number serves to give the weight as well as to identify the category. The letter also helps identify the category.

RULES FOR HOSTILITY DIRECTED OUTWARD CODING

1. Any given clause is scored only once for hostility directed outward. In cases where a series of verbs is used, the subcategory is assigned on the basis of the verb indicating the highest intensity. When a multiple object is used, for example, "I hate pets and children," the higher weight assigned to people, I*c*3, is given rather than the weight for subhumans, I*b*1.

2. The clause is *not* scored if the speaker alone is the recipient of the hostility.

3. When the pronouns "we" or "us" are used in a clause containing either an overt or covert hostility subcategory, the clause is scored. An example in the overt portion of the scale is "We planned to rob the store at midnight"—I*b*3. In this statement both the self (overt) and others (covert) are threatening the robbing of others, but the statement is coded only on the overt subscale. An example involving the use of "us" coded on the covert subscale is the statement "He threatened us with a gun"— II*a*3. Here one is confronted with both hostility directed outward (i.e., others threatening physical violence to others) and with hostility ambivalently directed (see Ambivalent Hostility Scale, below), but when using the Hostility Outward Scale, one will score the clause only in the context of others threatening physical violence to others.

4. In clauses containing "you" denoting a generalized form, the context must be consulted, since it is clear in some cases that the subject is really referring to the self as the agent and in others that he is excluding self and attributing the hostility-aggression only to generalized others. If the former case seems to be the accurate interpretation, the overt subscale would be applicable, while in the latter event, the clause would be scored in the covert portion of the scale.

5. In general, single words are not scored except in the subcategories: self or others using hostile words, cursing, or mention of anger or rage without referent (I*c*1 or II*c*1). Thus, words like "war" (used to designate a time), graveyard (utilized as a geographical location), fishing, etc., are not scored unless there is other evidence in the clause or immediate context of scorability. Do not score statements similar to "After the war, we took a trip to Europe"; "We flew over a graveyard"; "We went fishing this summer." Mention of "hunting," however, in whatever context is usually scored. It should be noted that this rule differs from the Anxiety Scale rule. In applying the Anxiety Scale, such words as "war," "graveyard," "morgues," etc., are ordinarily coded. On the Hostility Directed Outward Scale, they are not coded unless it is clear that such words are central to the meaning of the clause.

6. The idea of "abandonment" (see subcategories I*b*3, I*b*2, II*b*3, and II*b*2) is scored only if there is definite indication that

suffering or deprivation is involved. We are concerned here with the use of "abandonment" when it implies that the object has been deserted, forsaken, or somehow surrendered to the mercies or dangers of someone or something else.

7. While anything falling within the range of "injury" is generally scorable, it should be noted that pain, illness, and invalidism are not scored unless the sickness is of a traumatic type. Operations are scored only if they are obviously and/or permanently mutilating (amputation, hysterectomy, etc.).

8. In working with this scale, we have followed a convention of coding all hostility directed outward in red pencil or pen, so that it can be distinguished from other scoring.

EXAMPLES OF HOSTILITY OUTWARD

Overt Hostility Outward (I)

Self killing, fighting, injuring other individuals, or threatening to do so (Ia3)

SELF KILLING OTHER INDIVIDUALS OR THREATENING TO DO SO:

We are still manufacturing weapons to kill.
(They said) / I was the cause of his death.
I fought with the 12th Armored Division during the war.
I shot a boy.
I could have killed him.
I served in Korea during that fight.
(I dreamed) / I cut off their heads.

SELF FIGHTING OR INJURING OTHER INDIVIDUALS OR THREATENING TO DO SO:

I used to fight a lot with my sister.
We used to have great little rock fights.
They tried to get me to fight my best friend.
We'd all hit each other.
I started throwing rocks at my buddy.
(I told him) / I would slap him / (the next time he did that).
(I told him) / that I wanted to join an outfit / that fights.
I wanted to hit out at him.
We got into a fight at the corner drug store.
I was found guilty of assault and battery.
I hit her broadside on the side of her car.
I busted his ear a couple of times.
(They said) / I had threatened these girls.

I hit her in the head with a scrub brush.
I will give him a black eye the next time.
I wanted to stab her with the screwdriver.
I would have liked to have bloodied his nose.
We managed to really bruise them up.
(I was afraid) / I might hurt him.

Self robbing or abandoning other individuals, causing suffering or anguish to others, or threatening to do so (Ib3)

SELF ROBBING OTHER INDIVIDUALS OF THREATENING TO DO SO:

(I admitted / that was the car) / I stole the night before.
I used to sneak money out of her purse.
We decided to break into the corner candy store.
They caught me shoplifting.
When I steal their stuff / (they make me return it).
I'm in here for auto larceny.
(My dad told the officer) / what I was supposed to have stolen.
Then we were talking of burglarizing another place.
(When he wasn't looking) / I took his watch.

SELF ABANDONING OTHERS OR THREATENING TO DO SO:

(When I drink) / I don't even take care of my wife and kids.
(What kind of a mother am I) / that will sell her baby anyway.
(The welfare people are taking my kids / because they say) / I never am there / (when they need me).
I left her in the middle of the road and drove off.
(I knew / my buddy needed me) / but I was afraid to go back.
(I don't know) / what made me just leave my kids like that and run off with another man.
I gave up my baby / (as soon as it was born).

SELF CAUSING SUFFERING OR ANGUISH TO OTHERS OR THREATENING TO DO SO:

(She really screamed) / when I told her / (there were snakes in the river).
I hurt their feelings pretty badly.
(I knew / it would break her heart) / but I had to do it.
I am making my mom and dad pretty miserable about all this.

Self adversely criticizing, depreciating, blaming, expressing anger, dislike of other human beings (Ic3)

SELF ADVERSELY CRITICIZING OTHER INDIVIDUALS:

I started arguing all the time with Joanne.
Some ignorant nurse downstairs did it all wrong.

(I'm the only one in the family) / that can sue doc.
She was a mean teacher.
(If I saw somebody else doing that / I would say) / he was a hog.
She's a disgrace to our family.
He's a real charlatan.
I had a horrible teacher for that course.
She palmed herself off as a professional person.
My father was a brute.
He's completely unsuited for the job / he's in.

SELF DEPRECIATING OTHER HUMAN BEINGS:

He's not such a hot tennis player.
(I told him) / he didn't have the power to suspend me.
I don't think much of him as a driver.
(I said to him) / a little guy like you has to act little.
She's not so bright.
He's always kowtowing to others.
That's not a very smart doctor.
Anybody practically could do it better / than she did.

SELF BLAMING OTHER INDIVIDUALS:

It is his fault / (that things went so badly at the conference).
I wanted to get even with men by becoming a prostitute.
I'm going to haul her into court over it.
(It wouldn't have happened) / if he hadn't been spouting off again.
I kept accusing my wife of things.
If she'd learn how to park a car properly / (it would help a lot).
(I wouldn't have had any trouble) / if he'd stayed on his side of the street.

SELF EXPRESSING ANGER TOWARD OTHER INDIVIDUALS:

I'm pretty mad at all the boys in the club right now.
I hate everybody these days.
That turned me against him.
I told her to go to hell.
I started getting mad at him.
Sometimes I just push people around.
Sure I would get sore at them / (if they did things like that).
I despise them almost.
I knew / I might have to tangle with him sooner or later.
Sometimes I'd maybe curse them out.
I just sort of slaughter them verbally.

SELF EXPRESSING DISLIKE OF OTHER HUMAN BEINGS:

I never like / (the kind of person he is).
I didn't like / (the company I was with).

I felt an aversion to her from the very first.
The little brat's five years old.
(We told the boys) / we could not approve of their having friends (who act that way).
I didn't even want to try to get to know her.

Self killing, injuring, or destroying domestic animals, pets, or threatening to do so (Ia2)

SELF KILLING OR DESTROYING DOMESTIC ANIMALS OR PETS OR THREATENING TO DO SO:

I would like to kill that stupid cat.
I will be helping my father slaughter the hogs in the fall.
It was up to me to shoot the pony.
I squeezed my little mouse accidentally / (and it died of internal injuries). (The second clause is scored IId1.)
(The rabbit died) / because I forgot to feed it. (The first clause is scored IId1.)
(I told him) / I'd shoot his dog / (if it came in our pasture again).
I am going to call the Humane Society to help me put old Rover out of his misery.
The poisoned meat // I put out // took care of the cat / (that had been such a nuisance). (Ia2 and Ib1)
I just flushed our fish down the toilet / (when we left on vacation).

SELF INJURING DOMESTIC ANIMALS OR PETS OR THREATENING TO DO SO:

I kicked the dog / (as hard as I could).
I threw rocks at the dog / (every time it came in our yard).
In my dream, I seemed to be stabbing the horse.
I would throw that cat down the basement steps / (if I found it in the cream pitcher).
I accidentally cut the sheep / (I was shearing).

Self abandoning or robbing domestic animals or pets or threatening to do so (Ib2)

(When the kids got tired of them) / we just put the hamsters out in the backyard to fend for themselves.
We had to get rid of that dog too.
(I drove out in the country) / and just pushed the dog out of the car to get rid of it.
(When we left the kennel / I really felt) / as if I was leaving the dog in the lurch.
I teased the dog by taking his meat away from him.

Self criticizing or depreciating others in a vague or mild manner (Ic2)

SELF CRITICIZING OTHERS IN A VAGUE OR MILD MANNER:

I didn't like the type of clientele / they had.
Most of the guys in the fraternity are lazy anyway.
(It proved to me) / be careful of who you sleep with.
They are always late.
He sure had a weird sense of humor.
We were bickering about whether to have a party.
Some character just poked his head in the door here.
I don't trust him any more.
My kids sometimes get on my nerves.
We told her not to go so slow.
We never do get along too good.
He wasn't the kind of teacher / (I like much).

SELF DEPRECIATING OTHERS IN A VAGUE WAY OR MILD MANNER:

He's just good at making a big noise.
My dad isn't too mechanical.
That would be boring / (because it involves my husband).
She's never going to learn to knit at this rate.
(He always wants to help) / when it's too late.
(I think) / he looks like Gomer Pyle.
I'm going to ignore her.
He's sort of harmless as boy friends go.
My mother's kind of a snob.
He didn't know how to dance or anything.
He wasn't much use / (because he couldn't drive).
He was sort of peculiar fellow.

Self depriving or disappointing other human beings (Id2)

(I will tell him) / I want a divorce.
I quit at a bad time for them.
(On one throw I missed) / and I let my brother's knife get lost in the lake.
I ran my roommate out / (so I could have the room to myself).
I gave the officer a phony name. (That is, self depriving others of essential information.)
I forgot about taking care of the baby.
We went AWOL.
(I knew) / I had failed my husband.
I'm not sincere with my man any more.
(They felt left out) / because I didn't invite them.
(He tried and tried) / but I just refused him.

(I knew / she wanted me to take out the garbage) / and I didn't.
I have been neglecting my family.
I sort of upset them with my hours of coming in at night.
I just couldn't respond / (when my husband would come to me).
(I am failing three subjects) / so my mother is very disappointed.
(She's afraid) / we're going to ask her for something.
(I was aware / he wanted the house to look especially nice) / but I just didn't want to make the effort.
I let them down quite a bit.

Self killing, injuring, destroying, robbing wildlife, flora, inanimate objects, or threatening to do so (Ia1)

SELF KILLING WILDLIFE, FLORA, INANIMATE OBJECTS OR THREATENING TO DO SO:

I'd like to get a good three or four pound fish.
We went rat killing that afternoon.
(That was the first time) / I'd ever caught a really big channel cat-fish.
(It was snowing) / when we went deer hunting.
The flowers / (I picked) / died / (before I got them home).
I'll put salt on the sycamore stumps to kill them off.
I shot three squirrels and a crow that afternoon.

SELF INJURING WILDLIFE, FLORA, INANIMATE OBJECTS OR THREATENING TO DO SO:

I dented in the side of the car.
I shattered his windshield.
I knocked this little tree down / (when the car went out of control
I have to pay for scratching his car.
I broke the clothes line / (when I fell).
I just can't wait to throw that plant out.
We carved our names on the base of the statue.
We had a wreck with the car.
I tore a hole in my pants crawling through there.
We managed to rip a sail.
I burned a hole in the sofa.
(Every time I threw the knife) / it nicked the tree.
We were going to strip some bark from the birches to make things.

SELF DESTROYING WILDLIFE, FLORA, INANIMATE OBJECTS OR THREATENING TO DO SO:

We threw the dead rats off the bridge.
I tore the paper into a thousand pieces.
(When I picked the flowers) / they came up by the roots.

The car was worthless after my accident with it.
(The fish died) / after we threw that soap in the creek.
I crushed his toy plane accidentally.
The cup smashed to smithereens / (when I dropped it).
We stepped on all the ants to squash them.
(I wish) / I could rip that book to shreds.

SELF ROBBING WILDLIFE, FLORA, INANIMATE OBJECTS OR THREATENING TO DO SO:

I broke up the ant hill / (to see what they would do).
I took the eggs from the nest / (before the mother robin came back).
(I thought) / I would take the baby coons from the log / (while the mother was out hunting food).

Self adversely criticizing, depreciating, blaming, expressing anger or dislike of subhuman, inanimate objects, places, situations (Ib1)

SELF ADVERSELY CRITICIZING SUBHUMANS, INANIMATE OBJECTS, PLACES, SITUATIONS:

I have a couple of complaints.
He was the ugliest dog / (I'd ever seen).
Why should I spend money like this?
I hate dishes made of plastic.
Would it be an insult to the hospital / (if I went home)?
(Paddling is against the rules) / and shouldn't be done.
The milk isn't cold enough at the dining hall.
The car // (I bought) // didn't turn out to be any good.
Alaska is mostly a barren wasteland.
(I think) / this initiation period is kind of stupid.
Their food isn't fit to eat.
Getting badges in the Boy Scouts is just a farce.
It would be foolish to hold off any longer.
Talking into an empty machine is crazy.
It don't pay to work too hard.
We complain about that sometimes.
I didn't want to go swimming.
(I don't think) / any patients should have too much company.
This is an uncomfortable place.
It's going to be another messy day.
(I thought) / something was going wrong.
I don't care much for baseball.
It is awfully hot.
(I can't wait) / until I get out of here.
The water was a little too warm.
Television gets to be a bore, too.

SELF DEPRECIATING SUBHUMANS, INANIMATE OBJECTS, PLACES, SITUATIONS:

We didn't have a very good team.
The air conditioner doesn't work very well.
I like stupid things like comedians.
I would hate to make a living this way.
It wasn't much of a road leading back to the farmhouse.
The room smells bad.
Their apartment wasn't too well furnished.
This medicine doesn't seem to do much for me.
A dog like his couldn't compare to mine.
It was kind of "nyeh" as an experiment.
It's not much of a car / (but it may get us there).
This experiment doesn't make much sense.
It was more like attending a wake than a party.
I don't think it was worth it in the long run.

SELF BLAMING SUBHUMANS, INANIMATE OBJECTS, PLACES, SITUATIONS:

(They couldn't come) / because it rained so bad all week.
That intense heat is / what put us in such a lousy mood.
(I think) / the weather was the reason for the poor turnout.
(It didn't turn out) / because the recipe in the book was wrong.
(There wouldn't have been any trouble) / if the dog hadn't run into the street just then.
That particular intersection has always caused accidents.
(I told him) / it was the fault of the car, not the driver.
I blame those shock treatments for it.

SELF EXPRESSING ANGER OR DISLIKE OF SUBHUMANS, INANIMATE OBJECTS, PLACES, SITUATIONS:

I get kind of annoyed at television at times.
I can't take the heat too much.
I didn't like to have to be there very much.
(There's something about a tape recorder) / I don't like.
I don't want to scrub the toilet out.
I got pretty sick of the whole matter.
How many more times do I have to go through this tape recorder bit?
It was a lousy book.
The weather was foggy and dull the whole time.
(There are things) / I don't like about the club.
Isn't that awful?
That to me was just ridiculous.
I'm tired of loafing and lying around here.
This is a mess.
Just turn that tape recorder off for five minutes / (and I'd be better off).

What I didn't like was my back hurting me.
Turn that damn thing off.
I was wishing / the experiment was over toward the end.
(I don't think) / I've ever been so bored in my whole life.
I wanted to yank the electrodes off my head.
(I think) / that's unfair.
It was a trivial novel.
It's terrible to be idle.
There's too damn much preliminaries to getting into therapy here.
My brother and I ran away from the foster home.

Self using hostile words, cursing, mention of anger or rage without referents (Ic1)

SELF USING HOSTILE WORDS:

(I can't imagine) what in the devil / you want me to talk about.
Oh, darn it.
We just said the heck with it all.
I thought to myself, "Oh, nuts."
(It seemed to me), that everything was mostly crap, crap, crap.
I had a heck of a time getting home.

SELF CURSING:

There's no damn reason for it!
Why the hell am I here?
(I can't tell) / what in the hell is wrong with me.
It was just one damned thing after another.
Oh, shit!

SELF MENTIONING ANGER OR RAGE WITHOUT REFERENTS

I was so hateful all the time before my heart attack.
I learned the burden of hate working there.
I'm sometimes bad tempered.
(It's like) / I'm always furious at something.
(I don't know why) / I'm always angry.
(It seems to me) / like I'm just mad at the world.
I went around with a chip on my shoulder.

Covert Hostility Outward (II)

Others (human) killing, fighting, injuring other individuals or threatening to do so (IIa3)

OTHERS KILLING OTHER INDIVIDUALS OR THREATENING TO DO SO:

He fought with the 172 Division.
They killed about a million people during the war.
(I hope) / we don't have war again.

He's been sentenced to death.
Somebody might get killed / (when they pull those stunts).
The Sudan raids caused lots of trouble.
This is the anniversary of the bombing of Hiroshima.
The cowboys and Indians were shooting it up in that film.
His poor driving almost was the death of all of us.
(I feel) / this killing business is going too far now.
They shot those / (who could not walk).
He's up now for manslaughter.
That trouble all goes back to World War I.
The picture of the killer was in the paper.

OTHERS FIGHTING OR INJURING OTHER INDIVIDUALS OR THREATENING TO DO SO:

People are always willing to fight for their American heritage.
The story was about Morocco and the king and sword fighting.
They started into a fist fight with us.
He picks her up and throws her on the sidewalk.
They had a real brawl on the ward this morning.
All those integration riots were taking place there.
(We were afraid) / the Russians would capture us.
There was a lot of fighting during the football game.
He gave his brother a black eye.
One boy almost hit the M. C.
Her boy friend had beat her up.
They paddle the kids during their initiation too.
He hit the man on the back of the head with a brick.
Four boys beat up on the guy.
She gave him some pretty good lacerations.
(His dad told him) / he was going to break his neck / (when he got him home).
She likes to see Karen get a whipping.
(If they fell down on the march) / the guard kicked them.
He bit my little girl.
In Egypt at that time they were throwing acid in the faces of westerners.

Others (human) robbing, abandoning, causing suffering or anguish to other individuals or threatening to do so (IIb3)

OTHERS ROBBING OTHER INDIVIDUALS OR THREATENING TO DO SO:

They wanted to make off with a car.
A lot of the patients here steal things.
He stole one bike with this other boy.
The paper is full of robberies these days.
They waited till dark to break into the house.
She got his money / (while he was sleeping).

They had to steal bread from other prisoners to keep from starving.
(We knew) / they planned the job ((robbing)) for that night.

OTHERS ABANDONING OTHERS OR THREATENING TO DO SO:

He left her with absolutely no means of support.
He just disappeared and never came back to help them.
(If the prisoners fell during their work) / they were just thrown aside.
He put her out of the car miles from town.
She leaves those little kids all alone / (while she goes out with her boyfriend).

OTHERS CAUSING SUFFERING OR ANGUISH TO OTHERS OR THREATENING TO DO SO:

(He didn't care) how much suffering / he caused her.
The pledges are made to eat more or less nauseating things.
The Germans devastated Belgium.
She just made him miserable during their marriage.
She seemed to just do things to make her husband suffer.
He was always leaving her in tears with his mean behavior.

Others adversely criticizing, depreciating, blaming, expressing anger, dislike of other human beings (IIc3)

OTHERS ADVERSELY CRITICIZING OTHER INDIVIDUALS:

(He says) / he isn't going to sell to colored folks.
(They say) / she's a constant nuisance.
The police caught us.
They caught some men selling wine to patients.
They were taken to jail.
The police were after them.
Some college kids tried to stop a troop train.
He searched us for guns and stuff.
(They said) / they were poor examples of drivers.
He was put on probation.
He gave them all bad grades on their work.
Some boys got in trouble for doing that.
The police handcuffed her boyfriend before carrying him into emergency.

OTHERS DEPRECIATING OTHER HUMAN BEINGS:

They call them goddamned nuts.
My mother didn't think much of my friends in that crowd.
(They told him) / he was just a runt.
(She feels) / he is just small potatoes anyway.
(We were told) / that we weren't worth the trouble.

OTHERS BLAMING OTHER INDIVIDUALS:

He gave them a three-year sentence.
(The first year as nurses we thought) / everyone was going to sue us.
They accused us of it.
(She said) / it wouldn't have happened except for him.
(They tried to tell his parents) / he broke into houses and stuff like that.
He could have been fired for breaking the company rules.
We were sent to the Boys' Industrial School.
He got the blame / (whether he did it or not).
They all agree / it is mostly his fault.

OTHERS EXPRESSING ANGER OR DISLIKE OF OTHERS:

He picked on my mother a lot.
(I don't know) / why he doesn't like her.
My mother gets mad at him.
They really hauled them on the carpet that time.
My dad didn't like any of my friends.
He hates all minority groups.
The doctors should tell people // who are mentally ill // to get off their asses and get out.
She couldn't stand Catholics.
The Japanese were very hostile to Americans at that time.
The kids are all pretty mad at the teacher about it.

Others (human) killing, injuring, or destroying domestic animals or pets or threatening to do so (IIa2)

OTHERS (HUMAN) KILLING OR DESTROYING DOMESTIC ANIMALS OR THREATENING TO DO SO:

He just ran the dog right down.
He wrung the chicken's neck to kill it.
They wanted to butcher my favorite calf.
(I think) / she poisoned my cat.
(When the lambs are big enough) / they end up in the freezer.
They put the horse out of its misery.
She tries to poison all the cats in the neighborhood.
(They didn't seem to care) / that they were decimating all the herds that summer.
He drowns the kittens / (as fast as the cat has them).

OTHERS INJURING DOMESTIC ANIMALS OR PETS OR THREATENING TO DO SO:

The garbage man hit my dog with a belt buckle.
My sister might squeeze the cat too tight.

(People) who hurt dogs that way / (shouldn't be allowed to have pets). (Note: The clause in parentheses would be coded self criticizing others—Ic3.)
(He rode the horse through a pot hole) / and he broke its leg.
They were shooting their BB guns at dogs.
They tied a tin can to the cat's tail.
He knocked over the goldfish bowl.

Others (human) abandoning, robbing domestic animals or pets or threatening to do so (IIb2)

OTHERS ABANDONING OR ROBBING DOMESTIC ANIMALS OR PETS OR THREATENING TO DO SO:

They didn't seem to pay any attention to / what might happen to their pet mice / (if they gave them to the laboratory).
They let the hog struggle in the creek by itself.
My dad just abandoned our dog / and he drove away without really looking for him. (Both clauses are scorable IIb2.)
They left the kitten at the abandoned farmhouse.
(When the drouth became so bad) / they just left the cattle to find their own water.
She took all the puppies away from the mother dog.

Others (human) criticizing or depreciating other individuals in a vague or mild manner (IIc2)

OTHERS CRITICIZING OTHERS IN A VAGUE OR MILD MANNER:

They scrap with each other once in a while.
If they don't like / what we're doing / (we get demerits).
They're not too sure / (whether they'd like him for president).
The cop car started following them.
She fusses at him.
They would argue with each other.
The book told about the difference of opinion between Freud and Jung.
She wasn't very keen about his friendship anyway.
My husband picks on my younger son.
The newspaper editorial is sort of disapproving of him.
I found a lot of racial prejudice among them.

OTHERS DEPRECIATING OTHERS IN A VAGUE OR MILD MANNER:

(My parents thought) / maybe my date wouldn't make a good impression.
(She said) / they were just typical beatniks.
(His parents always feel) / he is too young for everything.

He usually called them krautheads.
They started calling people names.
(She thought) / he wasn't good enough for me.
They're always talking about the lazy, flabby Americans.

Others (human) depriving or disappointing other human beings (IId2)

OTHERS DEPRIVING OTHER HUMAN BEINGS:

They wanted to keep the Negroes from coming through.
They had their cigarette privileges taken away for a few days.
They never offer their loved ones anything.
We weren't allowed to talk or nothing all day.
He didn't support her.
They suspended his driver's license for thirty days.
Scranton tried to knock Goldwater out on the first ballot.
He got a twenty-dollar fine.
The boys were given only a little bit of milk as punishment.
She would never buy us nothing.
His mother never lets her decide anything for herself.
She won't ever try to help us or nothing.

OTHERS DISAPPOINTING OTHERS:

They were divorced.
He won't play with her / (if anyone else comes to be with him).
My mother had been separated from my father by then.
She didn't even offer my little girl any.
(My sister cried up a storm) / because my dad let her fish get away.
Her failure was a blow to them.
I guess / he lets his parents down over and over again.
She forgot to bring his books home for him.

Others (human or domestic animals) dying or killed violently in death-dealing situation or threatened with such (IIe2)

HUMAN OTHERS DYING OR KILLED VIOLENTLY OR THREATENED WITH SUCH:

The firefighter became a human torch.
More people get killed on the highways than in airplanes.
(It was the week) / that President Kennedy was killed.
(They called to tell me) / my daughter had just been killed.
It was really dangerous work.
One soldier was drowned in the mock battle.
We might all be blown up in a nuclear war.

(They were among the fleeing refugees) / when the strafing started.
Total nuclear war could destroy all mankind.
He never knew what hit him (bombing).
My boyfriend was killed August 7th.
I worried about her drowning.

DOMESTIC ANIMALS DYING OR KILLED VIOLENTLY OR THREATENED WITH SUCH:

My dog was killed by a car.
The cat was up in the tree / when it was struck by lightning.
During those dust-bowl years the cattle died like flies.
The poor kitten was smashed under the tractor wheels.

Bodies (human or domestic animals) mutilated, depreciated, defiled (IIf2)

HUMAN BODIES MUTILATED, DEPRECIATED, DEFILED:

They shipped the dead girl's body in a trunk to another city.
(They lined the box cars with / those who died) / and they sat on them. (The second clause would be coded IId1.)
The dead bodies were piled in heaps.

DOMESTIC ANIMAL BODIES MUTILATED, DEPRECIATED, DEFILED:

He stuffed the dead cat in a tin can.
The cars kept running over the dead dog on the highway.
The dead horses were just thrown overboard during the voyage.
They mangled the dead chicken.

Wildlife, flora, inanimate objects injured, broken, robbed, destroyed, or threatened with such (with or without mention of agent) (IIa1)

WILDLIFE, FLORA, OBJECTS INJURED, DAMAGED, OR THREATENED WITH SUCH:

We had a flat tire.
The toilet overflowed.
Lightning struck the side of the house.
The paint was peeling off on the walls.
There was a fire at the gas station.
The lining on her coat was torn.
That river is polluted.
He almost knocked over two gas pumps.
The storm blew the town apart.

The car started to skid toward the ditch.
She started slinging syrup all over the kitchen.
She chipped the platter.
I could hear the tire going down.

WILDLIFE, FLORA, INANIMATE OBJECTS BROKEN OR THREATENED WITH SUCH:

Boards, plaster, and glass fell over the room.
Those cookies crumble up in your pocket.
He tried to smash the window.
The catfish broke his line.
Some guy hit my car.
He rammed into the back of a car.
There was debris all over the place.
The bridges are being knocked down by the floods.
The vase was knocked to pieces.
Our television is broken now.

WILDLIFE, FLORA, INANIMATE OBJECTS ROBBED OR THREATENED WITH SUCH:

They would daze the bees with smoke before taking the honey.
They robbed the garden of its prettiest flowers.
The robin's nest had been rifled.
(The grass was dying) / because the great oak robbed the soil of all the nitrogen.
The bluejay took the worm away from the robin.

WILDLIFE, FLORA, INANIMATE OBJECTS DESTROYED OR THREATENED WITH SUCH:

The accident demolished the whole motorcycle.
My brother takes his boat and hunts and fishes.
He tore up the calendar page for the new month.
I'm going to talk about an oil-well explosion.
The test tube will blow up / (if that is done).
The plane was on fire.
(He managed to sink the boat) / so it couldn't be retrieved.
My brother broke the limb / (when he jumped on it).
Our house burned to the ground.
We looked around the junk yard.
She got a rabbit with her first shot.
All we have left is ashes, furniture ashes.
He killed two rats.
Most of the violets died.
It took him ten minutes to pull that fish in and gaff it.
The houses will be condemned for urban renewal.
The dock has been blown up.

Others (human) adversely criticizing, depreciating, expressing anger or dislike of subhuman, inanimate objects, places, situations (IIb1)

OTHERS ADVERSELY CRITICIZING SUBHUMAN, INANIMATE OBJECTS, PLACES, SITUATIONS:

He can't stand too much of this weather.
My parents don't like to have so much going on.
Goldwater voted against the bill.
(Some of the boys thought / the show was good / and some thought) / it was bad.
He always did take a stand against it.
They say the smog is pretty bad now.
Some of them disagreed with the decision.
He tried to avoid the situation entirely.
Henry Ford came out against it.
She is fed up with her job.
They thought / the cold was the most annoying part of it.
(He said) / the dog was badly trained.
(My mother thought) / the dress was poorly made.
(He realized) / New York was too crowded and dirty.

OTHERS DEPRECIATING SUBHUMANS, INANIMATE OBJECTS, PLACES, SITUATIONS:

Cincinnati didn't seem like much of a city to them.
Kids wouldn't care to live there.
He's not too interested in sports in general.
She doesn't care much for football.
(He thought) / the Navy couldn't compare with the Army.
(He thought) / the book was too frivolous.
(She said / when she'd seen one geyser) / she'd seen them all.
(She said) / dancing was a bore.
(My sister said) / that their dog was pretty scrawny-looking.

OTHERS BLAMING SUBHUMANS, INANIMATE OBJECTS, PLACES, SITUATIONS:

(I've seen) / some people blame something // that went wrong // on God.
Many people will become disgruntled with City Hall / (because the housing plans move so slowly).
(She said) / the apartment was too small for pleasant living.
(He thought / the plants were doing poorly) / because the room was kept so hot.
(My dad said / he wouldn't have slipped) / if the marbles hadn't been there.
(She thought) / the food looked so unappetizing because of the dingy china.

OTHERS EXPRESSING ANGER OR DISLIKE TOWARD SUBHUMANS, INANIMATE OBJECTS, PLACES, SITUATIONS:

(My dad saw that dog) / and he like to blew up.
He hated summer time.
His mother doesn't like bears.
My husband was mad at the idea.
They are really against all flying.
He didn't like the movie / (they were showing).
He and his buddy ran away from the reform school.
He despises all television shows.
They were always playing hooky.
She really hated that dress.

Others (human) angry, cursing, use of hostile words without reference to cause or direction of anger; also, instruments of destruction not used threateningly (IIc1)

OTHERS ANGRY, CURSING, USE OF HOSTILE WORDS:

He had an awfully hot temper.
They just seemed to be mad all the time.
She described herself as a hostile person.
He seemed to be furious.
They would always swear / (when they were drinking).
(He said) / he'd be damned / (if he'd go anywhere).

INSTRUMENTS OF DESTRUCTION NOT USED THREATENINGLY:

Other nations are testing bigger bombs.
We have some new missile guns.
My grandfather's favorite hobby was pistol shooting.
At the air ordnance, rockets and bombs are assembled.
I learned about loading guns on a tank.
We watched the atomic blast from a blockhouse.

Others (human or domestic animals) injured, robbed, dead, abandoned, or threatened with such from any source including subhuman and inanimate objects, situations (storms, floods, etc.) (IId1)

OTHERS INJURED OR THREATENED WITH SUCH:

The patrol brought the injured man in.
She fell and skinned her knee.
They brought her to church in a wheel chair.
The more dangerous the job, the more it pays.
The collision threw us both off of the motorcycle.
I recorded injuries and made out disability claims.
He just had some cuts and bruises and minor things.
It was an abdominal hysterectomy.

There are more accidents than there used to be.
He had his big toe cut off / (while he was mowing the grass).
He had lost his eyesight / (when he was a kid).
His pelvis was broken in five places.
The fish horned him.
He put a splint on the cat's broken paw.
The dog has gotten a bad cut somewhere.

OTHERS ROBBED OR THREATENED WITH SUCH:

(She said) / only her money had been taken.
His bike was taken during broad daylight.
(He reported) / that the camera had been taken from the car.
(They were afraid) / their house would be broken into.
(The mother cat wailed around) / because all her kittens had been taken from her.
(She locks up her purse) / so it won't be taken.

OTHERS DEAD OR THREATENED WITH SUCH:

They brought in the dead captain.
They never found Amelia Earhart.
My dad was attending his best friend's funeral.
Emily died on Ward F yesterday.
I read about the death of Marilyn Monroe.
A friend of mine passed away last night.
I wanted to attend my cousin's funeral.
The tumor was inoperable and malignant.
The little calf's mother was dead.
(I'm surprised) / we didn't kill ourselves.
"For the soul is dead that slumbers / (and things are not / what they seem)."
He gave her only three months to live.
The vet thought / my dog was going to die.
Some of the horses died during the ocean voyage.
The cat expired a little while later.

OTHERS ABANDONED OR THREATENED WITH SUCH:

Her daughter didn't come home that night / (and she lay on the floor all night / because she couldn't get back in bed).
"The band of exiles moored their bark on the wild New England shore."
The refugees had no place to go.
None of the farmyard animals would let the ugly duckling play with them or eat with them.
(They couldn't get out) / when the rising creek water cut them off from the main road.
(When the storm was at its highest) / they felt / they would probably never see land again.
They were typical exiles.

Subhumans killing, fighting, injuring, robbing, destroying each other or threatening to do so (IIe1)

SUBHUMANS KILLING OR DESTROYING EACH OTHER OR THREATENING TO DO SO:

(We watched) / the spider lure the flies and kill them.
The fish eat the mosquitoes and keep their numbers down.
The cat was a good mouser.
Sometimes mother hamsters eat their young.
That winter the wolves destroyed the flocks of sheep.
(If enough birds are around) / they will eliminate the bugs bothering you.

SUBHUMANS INJURING EACH OTHER OR THREATENING TO DO SO:

His dog gave mine a nasty cut.
The wasp stung its prey to daze it.
(You have to watch) / that the baby chicks don't hurt each other with their pecking.
The mother cat just bit her kitten's tail.

SUBHUMANS ROBBING EACH OTHER OR THREATENING TO DO SO:

(That bird never builds its own nest) / but it just steals from another species.
The deer were coming out of the forest and eating the hay put out for the cattle.
(My dog eats up his food) / and then he takes the cat's food too.
The squirrels are stealing the food / (they put out for the birds).

Denial of anger, dislike, hatred, cruelty, and intent to harm (IIf1)

I don't blame my wife for it.
I don't mind school so much any more.
I didn't want to have to fight him.
(Everyone knows) / I wouldn't hurt a kitten.
(I told him) / I didn't come to this hospital to fight.
It isn't that / I don't like him / (but things always happen).
I didn't mean to break her glasses.
I can't blame you.
It wasn't exactly your fault.
It wasn't bad at all.

Verbal Sample # 1 Coded for Hostility Directed Outward

Name of Subject:
   (Male adolescent delinquent)   Interviewer:
Date: Total Words: 211
Name of Study: Correction Factor: 0.4739

THE HOSTILITY DIRECTED OUTWARD SCALE

Well, this is going to be a story / about when I was out in the Children's Home. / Once we were doing something on bicycles / and the
            IIa3   Ic2
manager grabbed us and started to whip us. / And then I argued
             IId2
with him / so he made us all three stay in bed all day. / And then
                    Ia3
another time we was out in the park / and I was shooting arrows at
             Ia3
another boy. / I hit him in the cheek / so I got whipped again. /
      Ib1   Ib3
After that I just ran away. / Me and a buddy stole a car / but I got
 Ic3   IIc3
mad at him / and we split up. / But the cops got both of us anyway
               IIc3
and brought us back. / He got sent to the reform school then. / I ran
  Ia2   1c1
over a dog / while I was driving / and I didn't feel so damn good
         IIa1
about that. / Then the front tire got a flat / and that's / when they
caught me. / I hope / I don't get sent to any reform school, / cause
           Ib1
I'm pretty sure / I wouldn't like it at all. / Every day is just alike,
              Ia3
the same ordinary things / unless you get into fights or something. /
  IIa3   IIc2
They have a system of swats / if the boys do something wrong / or
       IId2
sometimes they take away their privileges. /

TABULATION OF VERBAL SAMPLE # 1 CODED FOR HOSTILITY DIRECTED OUTWARD

Correction Factor (C.F.) = 0.4739

Overt	Total weight	Covert	Total weight
$Ia3 \times 3$	9	$IIa3 \times 2$	6
$Ib3 \times 1$	3	$IIc3 \times 2$	6
$Ic3 \times 1$	3	$IIc2 \times 1$	2
$Ia2 \times 1$	2	$IId2 \times 2$	4
$Ic2 \times 1$	2	$IIa1 \times 1$	1
$Ib1 \times 2$	2		
$Ic1 \times 1$	1		
Total	22	Total	19
Raw score	10.43	Raw score	9.00
Corrected score (+ ½ C.F.)	10.66	Corrected score (+ ½ C.F.)	9.24
Square root	3.27	Square root	3.04

Total (overt + covert) = 41 × C.F. + ½ C.F. = 19.67
Square root = 4.44

Verbal Sample # 2 Coded for Hostility Directed Outward

Name of Subject:
   (Hospitalized medical inpatient)   Interviewer:
Date: Total Words: 215
Name of Study: Correction Factor: 0.4651

I was over at the Veterans Hospital for four hours this morning / and
                      Ib1
it sure was tiresome sitting in that chair there. / My back got pretty
sore. / My wife rubbed it for me / when she was in this afternoon
              IIb1   IId2
to see me. / She was complaining / because she still hadn't had any
word at all from our two boys. / Last week our insurance agent came
                      Id2
over to see me / and I told him to drop the policy on the one boy /
                                          Ib1
because he's not coming home any more / and what's the use of
                      Ib1
carrying it / so it's just a waste of money / and we can't afford it. /
      IId2   Id2
He never writes to us / and I told my wife / well we're not going to
write to him either. / They brought me wieners for dinner tonight. /
               Ib1   Ib1
Well you know them old wieners / I could never eat them. / They
                  Ib1
always rift on me. / I called the nurse about it / but but well, they're
                       Ic2
pretty slow in how they walk around here. / Well, well maybe Satur-
                                                        IId1
day I'll be out and can go see the boy / that was operated on for his
          IId1
eye. / I was sorry to hear about it. / Well it's just one of them things
                                      IId1
in life. / We don't know / what kind of an accident we may run
into. /

TABULATION OF VERBAL SAMPLE # 2 CODED FOR HOSTILITY DIRECTED OUTWARD

Correction Factor (C.F.) = 0.4651

Overt	Total weight	Covert	Total weight
Ic2 × 1	2	IId2 × 2	4
Id2 × 2	4	IId1 × 3	3
Ib1 × 6	6	IIb1 × 1	1
Total	12	Total	8
Raw score	5.58	Raw score	3.72
Corrected score		Corrected score	
(+ ½ C.F.)	5.81	(+ ½ C.F.)	3.95
Square root	2.41	Square root	1.93

Total (overt + covert) = 20 × C.F. + ½ C.F. = 9.53
Square root = 3.09

Verbal Sample # 3 Coded for Hostility Directed Outward

Name of Subject:
   (Female college student)   Interviewer:
Date: Total Words: 196
Name of Study: Correction Factor: 0.5102

Once my grandmother was very sick in the hospital / and I was supposed to go see her. / Before my parents ever got a chance to take me
                IId1   IId1
there / she died. / So I didn't get to see her / before she died. / I
        IId1
went to the funeral / but we didn't see her then either / because they
              IId1
had the casket shut. / And then, let's see / another time, one night a couple of girl friends and I went up to the N____ Club. / And there was this girl there // that we knew // dancing the Alligator with this
                        Ib1
guy. / It wasn't very nice. / And all these other guys kept egging her on. / And then the other night up at the N____ Club the police
                      IIc3
arrested two people, a boy and a girl, / and now the N____ Club
        IIb1   IIc3
is going to be investigated / because the police caught them serving
                        IId2
liquor to people / that were under 18. / They might have their liquor
                        IIb1
license taken away now. / My mother says / it's a terrible place / and she doesn't want me to go there any more. / It used to be a pretty popular place for kids from the dorm to go / when they finished working at the library. /

TABULATION OF VERBAL SAMPLE # 3 CODED FOR HOSTILITY DIRECTED OUTWARD

Correction Factor (C.F.) = 0.5102

	Overt	Total weight		Covert	Total weight
Ib1 × 1		1	IIc3 × 2		6
			IId2 × 1		2
			IIb1 × 2		2
			IId1 × 4		4
Total		1	Total		14
Raw score		0.51	Raw score		7.14
Corrected score			Corrected score		
(+ ½ C.F.)		0.77	(+ ½ C.F.)		7.40
Square root		0.88	Square root		2.72

Total (overt + covert) = 15 × C.F. + ½ C.F. = 7.91
Square root = 2.81

Verbal Sample # 4 Coded for Hostility Directed Outward

Name of Subject:
   (Male high school student)   Interviewer:
Date: Total Words: 186
Name of Study: Correction Factor: 0.5376

Well, usually in the fall on Saturday afternoons, nice sunny afternoons, my friends and I would go and play football / at this field we know. / I especially remember this one guy / who always stayed to block for the quarterback / and he really, he really knocked me down a lot of times. / He was playing fair / but he was putting a little
             $Ic2$
bit of extra into those those blocks. / And I remember trying to think
             $Ia3$
of some way to knock him down. / I didn't want to do anything
             $Ic2$
illegal / but I still remember really wanting to somehow get him. /
             $Ia3$
I tried a lot of times to make him fall down / but he would always
             $IIa3$
get me or one of my buddies knocked down first. / He was a sort of
      $Ic3$ $Ib1$
a mean-looking guy / and I didn't like this treatment / that he was giving me. / I finally thought / that that if I couldn't get through
      $Ic3$ $Ia3$
him / I'd at least make him look silly / but what I really wanted was
             $IId1$
to knock him down. / One of the other blockers got a bloody nose though / and we all stopped then. /

TABULATION OF VERBAL SAMPLE # 4 CODED FOR HOSTILITY DIRECTED OUTWARD

Correction Factor (C.F.) = 0.5376

Overt	Total weight	Covert	Total weight
$Ia3 \times 3$	9	$IIa3 \times 1$	3
$Ic3 \times 2$	6	$IId1 \times 1$	1
$Ic2 \times 2$	4		
$Ib1 \times 1$	1		
Total	20	Total	4
Raw score	10.75	Raw score	2.15
Corrected score ($+ \frac{1}{2}$ C.F.)	11.02	Corrected score ($+ \frac{1}{2}$ C.F.)	2.42
Square root	3.32	Square root	1.56

Total (overt + covert) = $24 \times$ C.F. + $\frac{1}{2}$ C.F. = 13.17
Square root = 3.63

THE HOSTILITY DIRECTED OUTWARD SCALE

Verbal Sample # 5 Coded for Hostility Directed Outward

Name of Subject:
   (Female psychiatric outpatient)   Interviewer:
Date: Total Words: 217
Name of Study: Correction Factor: 0.4612

                                    1a1
The only thing // I want to do // is / after I had the car wreck / I didn't know . . . / Anyway I got real nervous and sick / and I started
                  1c3
arguing all the time with my daughter / but I don't know / I seem
                           1a1
more close to her now / after I had the wreck / than I did before. /
                            IIc3
But the other kids, they always argue with her. / Naomi, my one
           IIa3   IIf1
sister, she likes to see Alice get a whipping / but I won't let them
          Ic3
whip her. / And then last night we got in an argument / because Billy got lost going after his sister yesterday. / And it wasn't my fault. / Don't know of anything else to talk about. / I don't know anything. / The little boy downstairs, Friday morning, I was washing. /
      Ic3   IIa3
Little brat's five years old / and he bit my little girl, / and I had to
                                IIa3
take her to the doctor. / He bit a big old piece out of her. / It was
  IId1   IIa3
just as blue / as it could be. / He bites everybody. / And then last
       IIa1   IIa1
Monday he tore the seat off her tricycle / and he stuck a knife in her
                              Ic3
toys, in her balls / that we buy her. / I never did like his mother, /
        IIa3   IIa3
she puts him up to that biting people. / I just told my little girl to bite him back. /

TABULATION OF VERBAL SAMPLE # 5 CODED FOR HOSTILITY DIRECTED OUTWARD

Correction Factor (C.F.) = 0.4612

Overt	Total weight	Covert	Total weight
Ic3 × 4	12	IIa3 × 6	18
Ia1 × 2	2	IIc3 × 1	3
		IIa1 × 2	2
		IId1 × 1	1
		IIf1 × 1	1
Total	14	Total	25
Raw score	6.46	Raw score	11.53
Corrected score		Corrected score	
(+ ½ C.F.)	6.69	(+ ½ C.F.)	11.76
Square root	2.59	Square root	3.43

Total (overt + covert) = 39 × C.F. + ½ C.F. = 18.22
Square root = 4.27

THE HOSTILITY DIRECTED OUTWARD SCALE

Verbal Sample # 6 Coded for Hostility Directed Outward

Name of Subject:
  (Female psychiatric outpatient) Interviewer:
Date: Total Words: 168
Name of Study: Correction Factor: 0.5952

Well there is only one problem at home, / that's my brother. / And
  　　　　　　　　　　　　　IIc3　　　　　　　　　　　　　　　　IIa3
his trial is going to come up in October, / he's up for manslaughter /
  IIa3
and that's / what's pressing on our mind and everybody else's mind
at the present. / And then the nervousness, I get awfully nervous /
  　　　　　　　　　　　　　　　　Ib1　　　　　　　　　　　　Ic2
and I can't stand to talk / I just can't stand people too long. / And
  　　　　　　　　　　　　　　　　　　　Ic3
sometimes I think / I just hate everybody except the children / any-
  　　　　　　　　　Ic3
body else I despise them almost. / I can't understand that. / So that's
  　　　　　　　　　　　　　　　　　　　　　　　　　IIf1
all. / Well, I'm not violent or anything like that, / only once that I
  　　　　　　　　　　Ia3
did hurt someone. / It wasn't / you know / it wasn't very bad / but
  　　　　　　　　　　Ia3　　　　　　　　　　　　　Ia3
I did do it / I did hurt someone that one time. / Well the only other
problem // I have // is the operation / that's all. / I hate having to
  　　　　　　　　　　　　　　　　　　　　　　　　　　Ib1
go into a hospital and that. / I don't know / what will happen to the
  　　　　　　　　　　　　　　　　　　　　　　　　IIb3
children. / My little boy's been taking things out of lockers at school /
and the principal called me about him. /

TABULATION OF VERBAL SAMPLE # 6 CODED FOR HOSTILITY DIRECTED OUTWARD

Correction Factor (C.F.) = 0.5952

Overt	Total weight	Covert	Total weight
$Ia3 \times 3$	9	$IIa3 \times 2$	6
$Ic3 \times 2$	6	$IIb3 \times 1$	3
$Ic2 \times 1$	2	$IIc3 \times 1$	3
$Ib1 \times 2$	2	$IIf1 \times 1$	1
Total	19	Total	13
Raw score	11.31	Raw score	7.74
Corrected score ($+ \frac{1}{2}$ C.F.)	11.61	Corrected score ($+ \frac{1}{2}$ C.F.)	8.04
Square root	3.41	Square root	2.84

Total (overt + covert) = $32 \times$ C.F. $+ \frac{1}{2}$ C.F. = 19.34
Square root = 4.40

CHAPTER VIII
The Hostility Directed Inward Scale

INTRODUCTION

The concept of hostility directed toward the self, which we call "hostility inward," has frequently been undefined or confused. Sometimes, it is not differentiated from hostility directed away from the self; at other times, it is regarded as a dispositional state rather than an ongoing experience. On still other occasions, it is equated with the syndrome of depression or considered to be the psychodynamic precursor of depression. And, quite commonly, it is used synonymously with the term "masochism."

Briefly, our Hostility Directed Inward Scale is designed to measure transient and immediate thoughts, actions, and feelings that are self-critical, self-destructive, or self-punishing (see Gottschalk *et al.*, 1963; Gottschalk and Gleser, 1969).

Validity studies indicate that the measure of hostility directed inward correlates with the psychological constructs of "depression" and "fatigue" as assessed on adjective checklists; the "depression" and "acute anxiety" scores derived from the Wittenborn rating scales (1955); the scores obtained from the Beck depression inventory (1961); and a clinical depression scale devised by Gottschalk (Gottschalk *et al.*, 1963). It measures a psychological construct *dissimilar* to that measured by the Oken hostility scale (1960) and other assessment procedures designed to measure anger or outwardly directed hostility.

The thematic categories of the Hostility Directed Inward Scale range in weight from one to four. A weight of one is given to statements about being painfully driven or obliged to meet one's standards or expectations, denials of hostility toward the self, or feelings of disappointment. A weight of two is assigned to verbal content in which the subject expresses a somewhat stronger feeling of deprivation, disappointment, lonesomeness, self-criticism, or self-punishing attitude. A weight of three is given to references indicating a greater degree of depression or more intense criticism of the self or references to self-injury. The strongest weight, that of four, is given to all references indicative of the speaker's desire to die or attempts (with or without conscious intent) to kill the self.

In effect, the categories $Ib3$, $Ib2$, and $Ia1$ form a subscale on the dimension of the self-criticizing the self. Thus for any statement in which the subject is expressing self-criticism (anger, dislike, depreciation) one makes a judgment regarding intensity; a very strong statement is scored $Ib3$, a less strong statement $Ib2$, and a mild self-criticism $Ia1$.

Since this scale, like our others, may be applied to language elicited in a relatively unstructured and permissive situation that provides minimal cues to the subject as to what spontaneous verbal responses are considered of evaluative significance, the subject is not given much opportunity to present himself in a distortedly favorable light. There is, thus, little opportunity for the message sender to disguise his feelings.

In the following pages of this section, the Hostility Inward Scale is presented along with the rules to be used in applying the scale (see Schedule 3). This is followed by a breakdown of the components of the scale listing examples of coded statements. As in the case of other examples listed in this manual, it has sometimes been necessary to include more than the coded clause in order to give the context within which it was decided to assign the score. Clauses other than those which are assigned the code have been enclosed in parentheses and/or separated by diagonal marks.

This section concludes with several one-page excerpts of verbal samples which have been divided into clauses and coded according to the Hostility Directed Inward Scale. The verbal samples are followed by tabulations of the scores, indicating the total raw score, the corrected score, and the square-root transformation.

SCHEDULE 3

Hostility Directed Inward Scale: Self-Destructive, Self-Critical Thoughts and Actions

I Hostility Inward

Thematic Categories

    a 4* References to self (speaker) attempting or threatening to kill self, with or without conscious intent.
    b 4 References to self wanting to die, needing or deserving to die.
    a 3† References to self injuring, mutilating, disfiguring self or threats to do so, with or without conscious intent.

Schedule 3 (*contd.*)

I Hostility Inward

Thematic Categories

b 3 Self blaming, expressing anger or hatred to self, considering self worthless or of no value, causing oneself grief or trouble, or threatening to do so.
c 3 References to feelings of discouragement, giving up hope, despairing, feeling grieved or depressed, having no purpose in life.
a 2 References to self needing or deserving punishment, paying for one's sins, needing to atone or do penance.
b 2 Self adversely criticizing, depreciating self; references to regretting, being sorry or ashamed for what one says or does; references to self mistaken or in error.
c 2 References to feeling of deprivation, disappointment, lonesomeness.
a 1 References to feeling disappointed in self; unable to meet expectations of self or others.
b 1 Denial of anger, dislike, hatred, blame, destructive impulses from self to self.
c 1 References to feeling painfully driven or obliged to meet one's own expectations and standards.

* The number serves to give the weight as well as to identify the category. The letter also helps identify the category.

† This code is reduced to a weight of 2 if the injury is slight. It is then written I*a$.

RULES FOR CODING ACCORDING TO THE HOSTILITY INWARD SCALE

1. The reference in a clause is *not* scored on this scale if it is clear that the speaker is referring to agents outside himself causing the criticism, injury, deprivation, suffering, or destruction. Such statements are to be scored on the scale of hostility ambivalently directed. If a statement is so ambiguous that one cannot easily ascertain whether the agent is the speaker or someone or something outside of the self, the clause should probably be coded on the Ambivalent Hostility Scale. An exception to this is the subcategory I*c*2—references to feelings of deprivation, disappointment, or lonesomeness—where the criterion for coding is the type of feeling expressed rather than the agent causing the feeling[1] (see also rule 4 below).

2. While, in general, one does not often find clauses scorable for hostility inward which have a plural noun or pronoun as the subject or object, such sentences do occasionally occur. Any clause that contains self-destructive or self-critical thoughts or reported actions is coded, even if a plural pronoun is used. For example, a statement of the type "We were really stupid to do something like that" is coded self adversely criticizing or depreciating the self (I*b*2).

---

[1] Consideration of whether a statement is verbalized in a passive or active voice is an important cue in distinguishing hostility in from ambivalent hostility.

3. In coding subcategory Ib2 (self adversely criticizing, depreciating self; references to regretting, being sorry, or ashamed for what one says or does; references to self as mistaken or in error), it is important that specific self-criticism be an integral part of statements of inability to perform or do something. For example, simple statements like "I couldn't cook well" or "I didn't know how to change the tire" are not scored unless they occur in a context which makes it clear that the speaker is actually criticizing himself or feels sorry, ashamed, mistaken, or in error. At times, such statements will be found in a context less of self-criticism than one of disappointment in the self. They are then to be coded in subcategory (Ia1), references to feeling disappointed in self or unable to meet expectations of self or others.

4. When coding clauses which contain references applicable to subcategory Ic2 (feelings of deprivation, disappointment, lonesomeness), the emphasis is on the feeling of the subject rather than the agent. This is, at times, a rather subtle distinction. It will be noted on the Ambivalent Hostility Scale (see next section) that subcategory IIa2 refers to others (human) depriving, disappointing, or misunderstanding the self. It is necessary, therefore, to distinguish the kind of emphasis which the subject himself gives to the feeling versus the agent. In a statement of the type "I wasn't allowed to play like other kids," the emphasis appears to be on the feeling despite the passive voice; whereas, in an expression like "My mother didn't even remember my birthday," the stress seems clearly to be on the agent.

5. The subcategory Ic1 has been included in this scale to cover references the speaker makes to feeling painfully driven or obliged to meet his own expectations or standards. Care should be taken to ensure that the clause, or the clause plus the context in which it is found, offer clear-cut evidence of this feeling. See the examples listed below for illustrations or statements coded in this category.

6. In assigning the code Ib2 to a clause, be cautious about scoring the word "embarrassed," for it does not always mean to be ashamed. Do not code "embarrassed" in subcategory Ib2 if it is used synonymously with any of the following: put out, encumbered, handicapped, impeded, upset, nonplussed, dumbfounded, disconcerted, or discomfited. For example, a statement similar to "So many questions embarrassed my naive mind" is not coded.

7. In subcategory I*b*2, the word "sorry" per se is not coded. For example, all of the following examples give references to the speaker being "sorry," but they are not to be coded as belonging in subcategory I*b*2. "I'm sorry / you're not feeling well." "Sorry / I can't get to your graduation exercises." "I'm sorry / you're upset."

8. In using subcategory I*a*1, context is important in the interpretation of statements such as "I failed in school." Do not score clauses of this type unless it is reasonably clear that the subject expects to do better or others have expected him to do better, and there is a specific reference to such expectations.

9. Category I*a*3—references to self injuring, mutilating, or disfiguring the self, with or without conscious intent—is multidimensional, that is, it includes not only the factor of degree of injury but also the factor of a conscious versus unconscious intent. When the degree of injury is slight, this code is assigned but the weight is reduced by one point (the procedure is somewhat similar to the convention used in the Anxiety Scale, where we increase the weight one point for evidence of increased intensity conveyed by comparative adverbs or by other means). When coding, the decrease in weight is indicated by a slash mark through the arabic numeral: I*a*3̸.

10. Hostility inward coding consists of a Roman numeral I followed by a lower-case letter indicating the subcategory and an arabic numeral indicating weight. A Roman numeral II prefaces coding on the Ambivalently Directed Hostility Scale, which is often coded at the same time as the Hostility Directed Inward Scale. We use a green pen or pencil for both types of scales to distinguish these hostility codings from those relating to hostility outward, for which we use a red pen or pencil.

EXAMPLES OF HOSTILITY DIRECTED INWARD (I)

References to self (speaker) attempting or threatening to kill self, with or without conscious intent (Ia4)

SELF ATTEMPTING TO KILL SELF WITH CONSCIOUS INTENT:

I cut both my wrists two years ago.
(I thought) / poisoning myself was the easiest way out.
(I thought) / I had taken enough lye to do the job.
I've tried to kill myself twice before.

SELF THREATENING TO KILL SELF WITH CONSCIOUS INTENT:

I want to take my life.
I've got suicide so much on my mind.
At one time I was even contemplating suicide.
I came mighty near jumping out the window of the hotel.
Sometimes I get an urge to kill myself.

SELF ATTEMPTING OR THREATENING TO KILL SELF WITHOUT CONSCIOUS INTENT:

(I didn't really know how to swim / when I jumped in the deep water) / and I started to drown.
I almost killed myself / (when the brakes gave out).
(I don't know) / how I happened to walk right in the direct line of the firing range like that.
I didn't pay any attention to the oncoming cars / (when I crossed the street).
(I dreamed) / I shot myself.
(I just wasn't aware of how many pills) / I took that night.
(I guess / I wasn't thinking) / when I stood in the bathtub and reached for the electric light plug.

References to self wanting to die, needing or deserving to die (Ib4)

SELF WANTING TO DIE:

(There are times / I just wish) / I could die.
(Sometimes I hoped) / I wouldn't come out of it alive.
(It was so bad) / I prayed for death to take me.
(I hoped) / one of the bullets would kill me.
I just want to end it all.

SELF NEEDING OR DESERVING TO DIE:

If I were to die / (my family would be happier).
(I don't know) / why God just doesn't take me off this earth.
(I didn't think) / I had a right to come through that battle alive with so many of my platoon gone.
I don't deserve to live.

References to self injuring, mutilating, disfiguring self, or threats to do so, with or without conscious intent (Ia3)

SELF INJURING SELF OR THREATENING TO DO SO:

(That was the summer) / I had a wreck.
I might injure myself / (if I walked 19 squares now).
(I know) / I bumped my head on the walls / (while I was on the psychiatric ward that time).

I got both my jawbones broken. (Notice that in this statement there is no mention of an agent other than the self. If the statement had read, "Both my jawbones were broken in the fight," it would then be scored on the Ambivalent Hostility Scale rather than on the Hostility Inward Scale.)
I slipped on the steps and broke my hip.
I fell off the bike and skinned my leg. (Coded Ia$)
I cut myself while slicing the meat. (Coded Ia$)
I ran track for a while and injured my ankle. (Coded Ia$)
(I felt) / like I been taking carbolic acid.

SELF MUTILATING SELF OR THREATENING TO DO SO:

I always bite my fingernails / (if I'm not allowed to smoke).
I scratched myself on the barbed wire fence. (Coded Ia$)
(The itching was so bad) / I scratched / (till I bled).
(I was so annoyed) / that I really lacerated my legs while shaving them.

SELF DISFIGURING SELF OR THREATENING TO DO SO:

(While I was messing around with my chemistry set) / I had another pretty good explosion / (and the iron particles got imbedded in my face).
I scarred my face from squeezing pimples.
I permanently disfigured my nose in that fight.
I sort of messed up my face doing that.

Self blaming, expressing anger or hatred to self, considering self worthless or of no value, causing oneself grief or trouble, or threatening to do so (Ib3)

SELF BLAMING SELF OR THREATENING TO DO SO:

(It's really obvious to me) / that I'm not easy to get along with.
It was mostly my fault.
(I found myself doing things with him) / that I knew were wrong.
(I know now) / how terribly wrong I was.
I used to feel so guilty / (when I did things like that).
(I guess) / I have a guilt complex.
I feel sort of bad about being so competitive.
I can feel the effects now of my wrong doing / (when I was younger).

SELF EXPRESSING ANGER OR HATRED TO SELF OR THREATENING TO DO SO:

I feel disgusted with myself.
I felt kind of stupid / (when everyone began laughing).
I'm still the same old stupid dopey guy.
(I feel) / that I'm the worst patient here.

Sometimes I hate myself for things like that.
I am my own worst enemy.

SELF CONSIDERING SELF WORTHLESS OR OF NO VALUE:

(I felt) / I was just a big failure.
I never seem to do anything right.
I just snarl up in everything / (I do).
Why would anyone want to be with somebody like me?
I'm just about ready for the junk heap / (I guess).
They were just idiotic judgments on my part.
I'm just a poor old uneducated man.

SELF CAUSING SELF GRIEF OR TROUBLE
OR THREATENING TO DO SO:

I'm just wrecking my own nerves.
(I guess) / I've created quite a bit of the trouble for myself.
My drinking is the ruination of my life.
I got to drinking moonshine whiskey and passed out on it.
(The life) / that I live / (may have caused all the tragedy / I had).
If I had come to the hospital right away / (I don't think / I would have been so worse off / as I was).
(I think) / my habit of worrying so much about everything is / (what caused me to have so much sickness).
(I should have known) / I was just bringing about my own downfall. (The first clause would be scored I*b*2.)

References to feelings of discouragement, giving up hope, despairing, feeling grieved or depressed, having no purpose in life (Ic3)

FEELINGS OF DISCOURAGEMENT:

(I feel) / everyone can be cured but me.
I never feel / like I'm getting anywhere.
I always end up back in the same rut.
There just isn't anything / (that I can do).
All I've had in my life is worry, worry, worry.
I'm discouraged this morning / (I guess).
I just can't hardly take it any more. ("It" refers to feelings about the self.)
His failure just left me disheartened.
(It seems) / like I'm never going to make it back to my old self.
I've had troubles all my life.

GIVING UP HOPE:

Life isn't worth living any more.
(It seems to me) / like every minute will be my last.
I just give up / (I guess).

(I guess / after a while I just realized) / it was too late for me to try to make a new start.
I ain't going to be here long now / can't eat / can't sleep.
(Even when I tried) / it was no use.
It's all too ... too much for me.
(I guess / my feeling about everything is just) / what's the use.
It might be two or three months / (before I die).

DESPAIRING:

(I feel) / I'll never be happy / (like I used to be).
I can't even stand myself.
(It seems) / like I'll never feel good again.
I don't know what to do about myself / (and what's the matter with me).
(It didn't seem) / as if anyone would ever help me.
I asked God to bring me out of my distress.
It was about the blackest time in my life.
(Talking ain't doing no good) / nothing is.
I've been despondent all day.

FEELING GRIEVED OR DEPRESSED:

(Her letter was so sad) / that I cried / (as I read it).
I've gone through a couple of severe depressions.
I felt pretty sad about that incident.
I get on these crying jags.
Sometimes I get to feeling so depressed.
I still have those downhearted feelings.
It was a terrible loss to me / (when he died).
I was in the dumps for a while around Christmas.
(They say) / I'll stop grieving by and by.
It's always the same old things over and over and over again.

HAVING NO PURPOSE IN LIFE:

I can't get interested in doing anything.
I don't know what to do except just sit here.
(It just doesn't seem) / as if anything means much.
There is no future to look forward to.

References to self needing or deserving punishment, paying for one's sins, needing to atone or do penance (Ia2)

SELF NEEDING OR DESERVING PUNISHMENT:

I turned myself in to the police / (because I knew / I had been doing wrong).
The reform school is my just desert / (I guess).
(I thought) / he was right to spank me for it.
(I guess) / I really felt better / (when they punished me).

PAYING FOR ONE'S SINS:

(If we have sinned in any way) / we should pay for it.
(I guess) / I'm paying now for all the wrongs / (I did).
(I guess) / I'll have to pay my debt to society.
Maybe that's why / I've had such a miserable life / all the things I did back then.

NEEDING TO ATONE OR DO PENANCE:

We must atone / (before we die).
I've repented everything / (that I can think of).
(I thought) / if I made myself do something / I didn't like / (I would feel better).
(I knew) / someday I would have to make up to them for all the wrongs / (I had done).
I wanted to make it up to him and be forgiven.

Self adversely criticizing or depreciating self; references to self regretting, being sorry or ashamed for what one says or does references to self mistaken or in error (Ib2)

SELF ADVERSELY CRITICIZING SELF:

Whatever I'm doing / I'm not doing it right.
I started going downhill after that.
I'm not totally rational about it.
I let myself go weak and got pregnant.
(I think) / I must have gotten up on the wrong side of bed this morning.
Sometimes I do a little bit too much.
I was terribly fat.
I cheated on myself.
(I know) / I'm crabby at home sometimes.
I smoke too many cigarettes.
I just get too drunk.
I am hard to get along with.
I think with no more light or anything / (than I did / before I had therapy).
(I don't eat all of it) / like I should.
(I guess) / I wasn't very tactful.

SELF DEPRECIATING THE SELF: [2]

My mind's not functioning right or something.
I have almost no sense of right and wrong.
I'm not much good any more.
The things on my mind are silly little things.

---

[2] This subcategory is to be used primarily in references in which the speaker describes himself in disparaging or disapproving terms.

I was a big flop.
I seem to be upset and confused all the time.
I went about in the same old flooky way.
My brain is messing with me this morning.
(I was afraid) / I might not make a good impression.
What little I know ain't worth telling.
My voice sounds so silly.
(I know) / I must look stupider / (than I am).

REFERENCES TO REGRETTING, BEING SORRY OR ASHAMED FOR WHAT ONE SAYS OR DOES:

I'm afraid / I hurt their feelings.
I shouldn't say this / (I guess).
(I wouldn't listen to my mother) / which I should have.
(Quoting prayer) Remember not the sins of my youth.
I tried to apologize.
I'm ashamed of the way / (I feel about them).
I want to confess it.
It wasn't very nice of me.
I'll apologize for it tonight.
(I could see) / that I had to quit drinking and start to straighten up.
I'm sorry / (I got so upset).
I confessed it to him / (when I saw him again).
Drinking seems to be my main problem.
(I know) / I wasn't supposed to buy the watch from my welfare money.
If I wasn't ashamed / (why would I refuse to tell people / what ward I was in)?

REFERENCES TO SELF MISTAKEN OR IN ERROR:

I had made a big mistake in my lifetime.
(I know) / that's wrong of me.
(I felt) / that I shouldn't get annoyed in that situation / (but I did).
I made an error in always overconforming.
I forgot the way.
I couldn't seem to get the right answers down, just wrong ones.
I always miss the right turn for this place.
(I don't know) / how I could have given such an erroneous impression.
(Tell me) / when I'm wrong.
I must have given her the wrong directions somehow.

References to feelings of deprivation, disappointment, lonesomeness (Ic2)

FEELINGS OF DEPRIVATION:

Sometimes I went all day without food / (it was so bad).
I didn't have a mother to talk to / (when I grew up).

I'm just a poor old goat with no money.
(She hasn't had any worse a life) / than I've had.
I can't seem to get close to my daughter any more.
My luck appears to have run out.
It wasn't a very bright situation for me to be in.
(If they keep on taking blood from my arm) / I won't have any left.
I never get a chance to do anything.
I'd give a whole lot to have a father.
I haven't had any breakfast or coffee or any of the things / (I'm used to).
I have to go home from the hospital / (and I'm still not able to do for myself).
I am not getting any Christmas presents or anything.
I haven't got a friend / (I could go to).
I didn't have a chance to go to school.
(I wish) / I could get out and go / as I please.
I lost everything during the flood. (Notice that while an outside agent—the flood—is indicated in this example, the statement is coded on this scale because of the feeling implied, i.e., "I lost.")
I have really missed TV since coming here.
I didn't have any relatives in that city to turn to. (This might be coded under the "lonesomeness" subcategory of this part of the scale rather than here, since both ideas are implied.)

FEELINGS OF DISAPPOINTMENT:

(I would have had a wonderful time) / if I'd only been well.
I don't get fun out of things any more.
I didn't get any mail at all today.
These old pills don't do me no good or anything.
I was so disappointed / (when I learned / she was married).
I don't make enough to really support my kids.
Our quarters there were quite a letdown.
I'm greatly disappointed regarding the church.
(My skin is always so bad) / that I never get a chance to go swimming.
(I want to go / but I'm sure) / I won't be able to.
(I expected the room to be filled for the meeting) / but only a handful came.
(I waited and waited for her) / but I never did see her any more.
Sure I was disappointed / (when he didn't stick around).
I miss the chance to go out for track now.
(I just wish there were some way / I could get to church today) / but I can't.

FEELINGS OF LONESOMENESS:

It's kind of lonesome being away from home.
(When I talk on the phone / I feel) all // I've got // is this little disembodied chunk of voice.

I have to be home all day long by myself.
Nobody cares for me.
I felt all alone / (when I didn't get to go to church).
Nobody knows / how I feel.
So now I'm very much by myself in the world.
I hate to be alone.
Maybe I'm just homesick.
I wish / I had someone to talk to.
I was very upset, very lonely.
I miss my children at times like that.
I have nobody to talk to most of the time.
Our stay at that hotel seemed rather friendless.
I get lonely at home at times.
I just feel forlorn / (when I'm with a group of people).

References to feeling disappointed in self, unable to meet self's or other's expectations (Ia1)

DISAPPOINTED IN SELF:

(I can't snap out of this feeling) / the way I want to.
I seem to be repeating myself over and over.
I just don't seem to know how to help myself any more.
I don't have enough education / (for the kind of work I like).
(I always dreamed of becoming a doctor or a lawyer) / but I never could make it.
(I always wanted to be a nurse) / but I don't have the proper training.
(I'd like to get back to work / because as it is) / I'm just not getting nowhere.

UNABLE TO MEET SELF'S EXPECTATIONS:

(I tried) / but I didn't make it.
I didn't even feel like combing my own hair.
(I thought sure / I'd knock in the runs in the game) / but I didn't.
(Although I worked at it) / my grades weren't too good.
(I found out) / I wasn't as bright in science / (as I thought / I was).
I'm not accomplishing much / (if I just rationalize it).
We hadn't done too well in spite of our efforts to make the group work.
(I wonder) / if I'm ever going to be independent.
I just don't feel right, laying in bed this way.
(I had been so sure / that it was a shock) / when I didn't get an "A."

UNABLE TO MEET EXPECTATIONS OF OTHERS:

I may run out of words / (and you'll be disappointed).
(It seems strange) / that I'm finding it difficult to find something to talk about for you.

I'm a total blank as to what to say for you.
(My mother was disappointed) / that I failed ninth grade.
(I've run out of anything to talk about) / I just can't keep it up.
(I tried to go on the diet / he gave me) / but then I couldn't.
(She brought me some sewing) / only I'm not able to sew now.
(They wanted me to go on to college) / but I couldn't make it.
I sure can't give you five minutes worth of talk today.
I am not able to talk for you today.

Denial of anger, dislike, hatred, blame, destructive impulses from self to self (Ib1)

DENIAL OF HATRED, ANGER, OR DISLIKE:

I've learned not to get mad at myself about things like that.
Before that, I wasn't hard to get along with.
I don't feel / (that I'm a complete failure).
It isn't / (that I'm ashamed of myself).
(I knew) / I had gotten completely over doing those stupid things.
I'm not going to hate myself / (just because the fraternity does things like that).
I wouldn't want to end up being my own worst enemy.
(I know) / I'm not the worst student in the class.

DENIAL OF BLAME:

I wasn't even in that neighborhood / (when the robbery took place).
It wasn't my fault / (she fell down the stairs).
(I knew) / I wasn't driving too fast.
I've never done no running around.
(I'm not going to take the rap for something) / I didn't do.
I've nothing to regret.
After all, I'm not the one who made the mistake.

DENIAL OF DESTRUCTIVE IMPULSES:

I'm glad / (that wasn't the end of me).
I'm not afraid / of what I might do to myself.
I don't want to hurt myself.
In general, I never did drink too much.
After all, it wasn't / (as if I was trying to break my leg).
I keep myself from thinking about anything / (that would pull me down).
I didn't want to get myself killed.
I ain't going to take any poison.

References to feeling painfully driven or obliged to meet one's own expectations or standards (Ic1)

FEELING PAINFULLY DRIVEN:

I worked too hard to get / (what I've got).
(I don't know) / why I make myself work so hard.
(They made it pretty hard for me) / but I stuck it out there anyway.
(I've always felt) / I had to stay home and take care of the children.
I pushed myself at work and at home.
I have to try to live with the things that come to me.
(I didn't sleep well / because I knew) / I had to get up.
(I felt) / I had to rush to get to the hospital this morning / (and it got me all worked up).
I'm going to try awfully hard.
I force myself to make my own definition / (of what is right for me).
How I was doing was on my mind all the time.
(I try to be as pleasant and nice) / as I possibly can.

FEELING OBLIGED TO MEET ONE'S OWN EXPECTATIONS AND STANDARDS:

(I never feel / as if I can go to class) / unless everything is completely learned.
(I try to keep as strong) / as I possibly can.
(After all, we couldn't invite them for dinner) / unless the house was in really apple pie order.
I don't want to miss a day / (when I'm supposed to come).
I always tried to do it to the best of my ability.
I forced myself to go on with carrying through.
I'd rather go to jail than be dirty.
If I can't be a perfect parent / (I'd rather not have children).
I keep trying to do / (the best I can).
I have to pick and choose my words very carefully / (if what I say is recorded or listened to).
(I always say) / "Be that labor great or small / do it well or not at all."

Verbal Sample # 1 Coded for Hostility Directed Inward

Name of Subject:
    (Male psychiatric inpatient)   Interviewer:
Date: Total Words: 237
Name of Study: Correction Factor: 0.4219

Well, in the first place, I've really tried to help myself / but I don't
    Ia1
seem to know how to do it. / It seems like / the things // I say and

108 THE HOSTILITY DIRECTED INWARD SCALE

          Ib2   Ib2
do // might be wrong. / Then I'd be wrong. / you know. / Cause
                      Ib2
that's all // I've ever done // is wrong things mostly. / And uh I
          Ia2
guess / I'm paying for it now. / (Long pause, subject weeping) I
                Ic3
don't know / what's the matter with me doing all this bawling. / I
                Ib2
was hoping / I wouldn't be messing up like this here. / Cause I want
              Ib1   Ia4
to be well. / I don't mean to drink so much. / That time when I took
           Ib1
the poison / I wouldn't have done nothing like that / if I hadn't been
    Ib2
drinking so long. / It was just too much of everything / and I didn't
               Ic3
know which way to turn anymore. / And I felt my nerves getting
                     Ib3
bad then / but they always do / when I stay up overnight. / As much
      Ib3   Ia2
wrong as I been doing / I guess / I just have to take / what the Lord
                    Ic2
sends me. / Maybe it all would have been different / if my wife had
                      Ia1
lived / and I weren't all alone in the world. / Maybe then I would
                   Ia1
have done more of the things / that I thought / I could do. / I could
have made a good mechanic / and I always wanted to / but somehow
      Ia1
I just never quite made it. /

TABULATION OF VERBAL SAMPLE # 1 CODED FOR HOSTILITY DIRECTED INWARD

Correction Factor (C.F.) = 0.4219

Subcategory	Total weight
Ia4 × 1	4
Ib3 × 2	6
Ic3 × 2	6
Ia2 × 2	4
Ib2 × 5	10
Ic2 × 1	2
Ia1 × 3	3
Ib1 × 2	2
Total	37

Raw score	15.61
Corrected score (+ ½ C.F.)	15.82
Square root	3.98

Verbal Sample # 2 Coded for Hostility Directed Inward

Name of Subject: (Male hospitalized
chronic schizophrenic)
Date:
Name of Study:

Interviewer:
Total Words: 189
Correction Factor: 0.5291

$Ic3$
Well, I can't put it in words / how bad I feel / how miserable I am. /
$Ic3$ $Ic3$
There's no future / I ain't got no future in here. / Nothing to look
$Ic3$
forward to. / There's nothing encouraging happens in here. / I don't
$Ic3$
know what to say now. / There's nothing encouraging or bright about
this place / it's . . . / I stayed here too long / but I realize / after
$Ib3$ $Ib3$
what I've done / they can't let me go. / It's my own fault / I guess /
that things turned out / like they did. / I call it temporary insanity
brought on by them seizures. / Wasn't for the seizures / I'd never be
$Ib2$ $Ia1$
in here. / My mind's going bad. / It ain't sharp / like it should be /
$Ib1$ $Ib2$
but I don't consider myself insane. / It's just that your mind gets
rusty. / I get tired of these interviews, just talking. / What you say
$Ic2$ $Ic2$
don't amount to anything anyway. / Complaints don't mean any-
$Ic2$
thing. / You've got no rights by law. / They do as they damn please
$Ic3$ $Ic3$
with you. / See no hopes of getting out of here. / I expect to spend
my life here. / They could make a hell of a lot of improvements
around here / if they would. /

*TABULATION OF VERBAL SAMPLE # 2 CODED FOR
HOSTILITY DIRECTED INWARD*

Correction Factor (C.F.) = 0.5291

Subcategory	Total weight
$Ib3 \times 2$	6
$Ic3 \times 7$	21
$Ib2 \times 2$	4
$Ic2 \times 3$	6
$Ia1 \times 1$	1
$Ib1 \times 1$	1
Total	39

Raw score	39
Corrected score (+ ½ C.F.)	20.90
Square root	4.57

THE HOSTILITY DIRECTED INWARD SCALE

Verbal Sample # 3 Coded for Hostility Directed Inward

Name of Subject:
  (Male psychiatric outpatient)
Date:
Name of Study:

Interviewer:
Total Words: 219
Correction Factor: 0.4566

Well I've been nervous all my life. / I've said and done a lot of things
                                                                      $Ib2$
to my wife, accused her / things that weren't true. / I would go out
and drink, and but but / when I would do that / I'd come back and
                        $Ib2$ $Ib2$
tell her / I'm sorry / and I meant it. / And maybe she would let this
                                  $Ib2$
go by / and I'd do it again / and I'm sorry all over. / And then it
got to a place / where she didn't care / what I would say and and
                                       $Ib3$
my my feelings at all / but I figures / well I deserved that / because
                                   $Ib2$
I'd been so mean. / But then I tried to make up with her / and she
says / she just hates me. / And it's just driving me crazy, / I just
can't eat or sleep, / I'm nervous. / I work / but I can't hardly stand
anything. / And I'll go and get a few beers / and maybe I stumble
                            $Ia3$* $Ic2$
and skin myself up on the way home. / Because I'll be all alone /
when I do get home. / And then I know / through the years I've, /
                $Ib3$
it's been my fault. / I'm coming here hoping to please her / because
                     $Ic3$ $Ic3$
I love her. / I'd be crying like a baby. / I can't help it. / Now she
                                          $Ib1$ $Ib1$
blames me / because I punished the kid. / But I didn't / I didn't do
that. /

TABULATION OF VERBAL SAMPLE # 3 CODED FOR HOSTILITY DIRECTED INWARD

Correction Factor (C.F.) = 0.4566

Subcategory	Total weight
$Ia3$* × 1	2
$Ib3$ × 2	6
$Ic3$ × 2	6
$Ib2$ × 5	10
$Ic2$ × 1	2
$Ib1$ × 2	2
Total	28

Raw score   12.78
Corrected score (+ ½ C.F.)   13.01
Square root   3.61

* Note that score is reduced by one to indicate minor injury.

THE HOSTILITY DIRECTED INWARD SCALE 111

Verbal Sample # 4 Coded for Hostility Directed Inward

Name of Subject:
   (Female psychiatric outpatient)   Interviewer:
Date: Total Words: 167
Name of Study: Correction Factor: 0.5988

                                                        $Ia4$

Not a very good subject. / (6 words) / I just feel like killing myself. / I've got four children, / but what's (word) that. / They'll grow up / and they leave. / Then I think / about what kind of woman,
                                                                      $Ib3$

what kind of mother am I / that will do the things / that I've done. / I don't know / just without my husband as far as I'm concerned /
      $Ic3$

there's no life. / And when I get drinking / I do need help, / any-
                     $Ia4$

body who wants to kill theirself. / And I'd like to know / where I
                               $Ib3$

failed my husband at / why made him / he turn to another woman. / He was that way for seven months. / I found out a month ago / he was living with another woman. / The whole time he said / I drove him to it. / Anything // he does / he thinks // is all right. / But I
                         $Ib2$

go out and make one mistake / and that's it. / He asked me / if I'd put the baby up for adoption / and I did. / Now I know / I was
   $Ib2$ $Ic2$

wrong. / Now I got nothing. /

TABULATION OF VERBAL SAMPLE # 4 CODED FOR
HOSTILITY DIRECTED INWARD

Correction Factor (C.F.) = 0.5988

Subcategory	Total weight
$Ia4 \times 2$	8
$Ib3 \times 2$	6
$Ic3 \times 1$	3
$Ib2 \times 2$	4
$Ic2 \times 1$	2
Total	23

Raw score   13.77
Corrected score (+ ½ C.F.)   14.07
Square root   3.75

Verbal Sample # 5 Coded for Hostility Directed Inward

Name of Subject:
   (Female psychiatric outpatient)   Interviewer:
Date: Total Words: 214
Name of Study: Correction Factor: 0.4673

112 THE HOSTILITY DIRECTED INWARD SCALE

Well . . . I was a young girl / my father and mother was poor. /
$\qquad$ Ic2
They could not send me to school / and we had an awful hard life. /
$\qquad$ Ic2
We didn't get no education hardly / so I've had it pretty hard in my
$\qquad$ Ib2
life. / So that's all / I can say, think to say. / I know / I'm silly, real
$\qquad$ Ib1
silly, / but I know / I'm not bad or crazy or anything like that. /
Things make me all upset / and then I lay awake at night / and I
$\qquad$ Ic1
think about all the things piled up / that I've just got to get done the
$\qquad$ Ic1
next day / or I think / about the places I've got to go to. / I can't
$\qquad$ Ib2
stand for nobody to bawl me out. / That's my worst fault / I think. /
When somebody speaks loud to me or bawls me out / I just can't
$\qquad$ Ib2
stand it. / And I know / I've been thinking more or less selfish / and
$\qquad$ Ia1 $\qquad$ Ic2
I've sort of fumbled my way through life. / But I never got the edu-
$\qquad$ Ib2
cation / I needed and wanted / and I just made lots of mistakes and
$\qquad$ Ic2
blunders along the way. / I've never had a time / when I just had
$\qquad$ Ic2
good times. / I've always had to do without and make things do. /
$\qquad$ Ic1
But I've tried / as hard and as best as I possibly could. /

TABULATION OF VERBAL SAMPLE # 5 CODED FOR
HOSTILITY DIRECTED INWARD

Correction Factor (C.F.) = 0.4673

Subcategory	Total weight
$Ib2 \times 4$	8
$Ic2 \times 5$	10
$Ia1 \times 1$	1
$Ib1 \times 1$	1
$Ic1 \times 3$	3
Total	23

Raw score 10.75
Corrected score (+ ½ C.F.) 10.98
Square root 3.32

THE HOSTILITY DIRECTED INWARD SCALE

Verbal Sample # 6 Coded for Hostility Directed Inward

Name of Subject:
  (Female psychiatric inpatient)   Interviewer:
Date: Total Words: 210
Name of Study: Correction Factor: 0.4762

I love my husband very much / and I hope / that he loves me / and I want to get well. / I, I want to get over this fear / that I have. /
                                                                                        $Ic2$
And I want to get home / as soon as I can. / I miss my family / when I have to stay here. / I can't think of anything else right
                                $Ib2$ $Ib2$
now. / That's not very interesting / is it. / But then I'm not a very interesting person. / My, I'm all mixed up. / My mind's not func-
                              $Ib2$
tioning right or something. / So I don't know. / I don't . . . / I've had a pretty, // I mean // a hectic life. / Nothing much ever hap-
                                                                                            $Ic2$
pened to me / just that I had a lot of ups and downs, many disap-
                                                              $Ib2$
pointments and regrets also. / Regrets of many many years, over
                             $Ic2$ $Ic2$
many years. / That I can't go back / but I wish / I could. / But I
                            $Ib3$ $Ib3$
can't / and this is / where I ended up. / I seem to be my own worst enemy. / But there's two sides to every story, to everything. / And
                                                                     $Ic3$
I guess / I'm just practically at the end of my rope these days. / I
               $Ic3$ $Ic2$
don't know where to turn now. / I've had good years and miserable
                                             $Ic3$
years / and now I just have miserable years. / But nothing special has ever happened in my life. /

TABULATION OF VERBAL SAMPLE # 6 CODED FOR HOSTILITY DIRECTED INWARD

Correction Factor (C.F.) = 0.4762

Subcategory	Total weight
$Ib3 \times 2$	6
$Ic3 \times 3$	9
$Ib2 \times 4$	8
$Ic2 \times 5$	10
Total	33

Raw score   15.71
Corrected score (+ ½ C.F.)   15.95
Square root   3.99

CHAPTER IX
The Ambivalent Hostility Scale

INTRODUCTION

Verbal statements scored on the Ambivalent Hostility Scale are all themes about destructive, injurious, critical thoughts and actions of others (including situations and objects) toward the self. Our construct of ambivalent hostility pertains to statements by the speaker concerning hostility directed to him from sources outside himself. It consequently overlaps to some extent the constructs of both hostility directed inward and hostility directed outward, particularly the overt portion of the Hostility Outward Scale.

A discussion of the development of this scale and references to studies relating to its reliability and validity will be found elsewhere (Gottschalk *et al.*, 1963; Gottschalk and Gleser, 1969).

As in the other two hostility scales, the Ambivalent Hostility Scale assigns higher weights to scorable verbal statements communicating hostility that, by inference, is more likely to be strongly experienced by the speaker than that which is relatively outside his awareness. The weights assigned to content categories range from a numerical value of one (given either to denial of blame or to subhuman or inanimate agents acting hostilely toward the self) to a value of three (given to the four subcategories at the upper end of the scale which culminate in some other human attempting or threatening to kill the self).

This section provides the following information:

1. A description of the Ambivalent Hostility Scale (Schedule 4). When coding verbal samples for ambivalent hostility, the code is prefaced by a Roman numeral II (distinguishing this scale from the Hostility Inward Scale, which is prefaced with a Roman numeral I); the content subcategory is then given in a lower-case letter and is followed by the weight in an arabic numeral.

2. The specific rules pertinent to the use of the Ambivalent

Hostility Scale. General rules applicable to all scales are found in an earlier section.

3. Step-by-step breakdown of the components of the scale and examples of the various subcategories.

4. Excerpts of verbal samples. Diagonal marks are used to indicate the clauses, and the scoring for codable clauses is shown. The scores of the coded verbal samples are shown in tabular form, and the conversion from raw score to corrected score to square-root transformation is provided.

SCHEDULE 4

Ambivalent Hostility Scale: Destructive, Injurious, Critical Thoughts and Actions of Others to Self

II Ambivalent Hostility

Thematic Categories

a 3* Others (human) killing or threatening to kill self.
b 3 Others (human) physically injuring, mutilating, disfiguring self or threatening to do so.
c 3 Others (human) adversely criticizing, blaming, expressing anger or dislike toward self or threatening to do so.
d 3 Others (human) abandoning, robbing self, causing suffering, anguish, or threatening to do so.
a 2 Others (human) depriving, disappointing, misunderstanding self or threatening to do so.
b 2 Self threatened with death from subhuman or inanimate object, or death-dealing situation.
a 1 Others (subhuman, inanimate, *or situation*), injuring, abandoning, robbing self, causing suffering, anguish.
b 1 Denial of blame.

* The number serves to give the weight as well as to identify the category. The letter also helps identify the category.

RULES FOR AMBIVALENT HOSTILITY CODING

1. Only one score is assigned to any given clause on this scale, although the same clause may be coded for some other affect as measured by the anxiety or other hostility scales.

2. There appear to be many instances of hostility directed toward the self occurring in the content of verbal samples in which it is not clear whether the speaker is the agent (and the content should be coded for hostility inward) or the agent is seen as something outside of oneself (and the content should then be coded for ambivalent hostility). While the clause in and of itself may not give one this information, it is frequently possible from the immediate context of the clause to determine the extent to which the

speaker feels he is a passive entity being acted upon in contrast to seeing himself as an active agent. In general, however, if the person scoring feels that real ambiguity exists as to whether a reference is to be coded on one or the other of these two scales, the choice should be made in favor of the Ambivalent Hostility Scale.

As noted in rules for the Hostility Inward Scale, however, an exception to this is made in the case of references to the self being deprived, disappointed, or lonesome. Such statements fall into the Ambivalent Hostility Scale only when the outside agent is definitely and unmistakably mentioned and it is clear that the agent is as or more important than the feeling being described. (See examples illustrating the distinction between these two subcategories below in IIa2 under others (human) depriving, disappointing, misunderstanding self, as well as above in Ic2 in the Hostility Inward Scale.)

3. Subcategory IId3 contains references to the idea of being abandoned. One should be careful in assigning this score to a clause that the abandonment actually causes suffering. Simple statements of the type "We were laid off from our jobs" are not interpreted as abandonment unless the context clearly indicates that the speaker has actually felt deserted or abandoned.

4. Subcategory IIa1 includes the concept of "situation" along with subhuman or inanimate others as the agent causing injury or abandonment, robbing the self, or causing suffering or anguish. The "situations" can include those arising from agents external to the self and those which are ambiguous, that is, which cannot be attributed specifically to the self.

5. In general, when the content indicates that "others" make the speaker worried, upset, bothered, concerned, etc., care must be exercised by the coder to ensure that more affect appears to be communicated than in similar content which would be scorable on the Anxiety Scale. If in doubt as to whether ambivalent hostility is present, do not score. If, however, the speaker does in effect seem to be saying that he sees others as behaving in some sort of hostile fashion to him resulting in his feeling of anxiety-fear, consideration is given to subcategory IIa2 of the Ambivalent Hostility Scale, that is, others (human) depriving, disappointing, misunderstanding the self or threatening to do so, rather than the more heavily weighted IId3.

6. Although the clause "I got into trouble" is verbalized in an active rather than a passive form, it is our practice—when the context leaves us in doubt—to score the content of this clause for ambivalent hostility rather than for hostility directed inward. Most of the rather large number of verbal samples we have collected using this statement come from lower socioeconomic class groups: patients coming to a municipal general hospital, persons referred to a municipal psychiatric court clinic in connection with difficulties with the law, or juvenile delinquents. We have found that when subjects of these groups refer to "getting into trouble," they are usually making statements about the hostility of others to them rather than being critical of the self. Walter B. Miller (1962) has reported similar observations from his studies of the cultures of the lower socioeconomic classes. Of course, when the context leaves no doubt that hostility directed inward is being expressed, then such a statement is classified as communicating inward hostility.

7. If one is coding on all three hostility scales, note that all statements of the kind "They criticized us" will be coded both on the covert portion of the Hostility Directed Outward Scale (others hostile to others) and on the Ambivalently Directed Hostility Scale (others critical of or injurious to the self). Specifically, whenever the object of hostility includes the self and the nonself, the reference is coded on both scales.

8. In general, it has been convenient and helpful in maintaining good coding reliability to score content on the hostility inward and the ambivalent hostility measures at the same time. We have followed the convention of scoring both in green pencil or green pen and identifying the ambivalent hostility with a Roman numeral II to distinguish such coding from hostility inward, which is prefaced with a Roman numeral I.

EXAMPLES OF AMBIVALENTLY DIRECTED HOSTILITY (II)

Others (human) killing or threatening to kill self (IIa3)

(I think) / he would have killed me.
(I was afraid) / that he might shoot me in the back.
When the Germans strafed our platoon / (some of the men ran).
(That was the time / I dreamed) / she was going to drown me.
The Japanese shore guns opened up on us.
She is threatening to shoot me.

Others (human) physically injuring, mutilating, disfiguring self or threatening to do so (IIb3)

OTHERS PHYSICALLY INJURING THE SELF OR THREATENING TO DO SO:

In my dream he told me to take a teaspoon of carbolic acid.
At that point she jumped at me and hit me.
What a blow he gave me.
He ran after us with a broom.
She keeps jabbing me with that needle.
The patient in the next bed struck out at me.
(I don't know) / what he may try to do next to hurt me.
My parents used to give me a good whipping for things like that.

OTHERS MUTILATING OR DISFIGURING THE SELF OR THREATENING TO DO SO:

The boys scratched me in the melee.
I am afraid / he is going to scar up my face.
(He said) / he'd like to make mincemeat of me.
In my dream they had left a horrible tattoo on my forehead.

Others (human) adversely criticizing, blaming, expressing anger or dislike toward the self or threatening to do so (IIc3)

OTHERS ADVERSELY CRITICIZING THE SELF OR THREATENING TO DO SO:

They were jealous of my working so much, putting out so much work.
(I was sure) / she had said something nasty about me.
None of her family liked my drinking.
(He told me) / my work had not been satisfactory.
My children are very disgusted with me.
They were always calling me fat or something.
(I know / you think) / I'm stupid.
She might bawl me out for that.

OTHERS BLAMING THE SELF OR THREATENING TO DO SO:

The cop gave me a ticket for a parking violation.
Both my friends lit into me about my interfering with them.
Then they put me in jail.
Maybe the law is trying to find out about me.
(That was the time) / I got in trouble.
My daughter got after me / (because I had forgotten it).
(They are going to say) / it was all my fault.
(My dad thought) / I was the only culprit.

OTHERS EXPRESSING ANGER OR DISLIKE TOWARD THE SELF OR THREATENING TO DO SO:

They made it pretty hostile for me to be there.
They won't even speak to me.
Consider my enemies / for they are many / and they hate me with cruel hate. (Three scores of IIc3)
She always just brushed me aside more or less.
I must have enemies up here somewhere.
My mother told me to pack my clothes and get out.
The doctor was really furious at me.
They are going to hate me for doing that.
The principal would have been pretty mad at us / (if he had learned about that escapade).

Others (human) abandoning, robbing self, causing suffering or anguish, or threatening to do so (IId3)

OTHERS ABANDONING SELF OR THREATENING TO DO SO:

They kicked me out of Cincinnati.
Ain't none of them doctors come to see me any more.
(They say) / that my mother just left me and never came back.
They're just going to let me die here in a corner or something.
(I feel) / as though he is going to throw me to the wolves.
They just let me lie here all alone.
In my dream, my wife vanished away and left me there alone again, by myself.
(If you're not a white collar man) / you're not wanted.
(I'm afraid) / they might discharge me / (if I make these complaints).

OTHERS ROBBING SELF OR THREATENING TO DO SO:

He even steals my cigarettes.
My brother and his buddy still take all my money.
My car was broken into during commencement.
They managed to get my wallet.
They would have gotten my ring / (if they could).
Somehow she always manages to steal my boy friend away.

OTHERS CAUSING SUFFERING OR ANGUISH OR THREATENING TO DO SO:

"Let not my enemies tramp over me."
(When you first go out there) / the boys give you a pretty bad time.
She wanted to take us back to the reform school / (so we ran / while she was phoning).
(I'm so sick) / please don't keep bothering and bothering me.

(I think) / they drugged me.
(It's a downright shame) / the way some people treat me here.
Hospitals can make it miserable for you too.
He was always causing me some kind of heartbreak.
Unhappiness and a loused up life was all / (he did for me).

Others (human) depriving, disappointing, misunderstanding self or threatening to do so (IIa2)

OTHERS DEPRIVING SELF OR THREATENING TO DO SO:

(While I was there / the plant closed) / and everybody had to leave.
My probation officer wouldn't let me have the letter from my girl friend.
Now they probably won't bring my lunch back / (until it's all cold).
They're going to take away my campus parking privileges.
They borrowed my money and never paid it back.
(Our parents decided) / we'd all have to do without our allowance for a month.
(My sister's condition is) / what keeps on holding me down all the time.
My nieces and nephews, they don't do anything for me any more.
The gas and electric company just turn everything off on you / (if you can't pay on the dot).
They never want to let me do anything.
You're wasting my time with this research stuff.
The nurse wouldn't let me read late at night.
You don't do / (like I ask you to do).
Our house parents cut out our after-supper smoking.

OTHERS DISAPPOINTING SELF OR THREATENING TO DO SO:

I don't get much help out of either of my kids.
Nothing they do seems to help me.
(I waited for you) / and you never did show up.
(When I need him) / he's never there.
They (hospital personnel) ain't going to do nothing for me nohow.
She never comes to see me / (and I know / she could).
They didn't give me anything but that one treatment.
(I thought / she would promote me) / but she didn't.
(She was supposed to come back to see me) but she forgot to.
They must have forgotten to pick me up for the movie.
My wife didn't show up again last night.
My parents never keep their promises.
If my son doesn't want to write / (we're not going to either).

OTHERS MISUNDERSTANDING THE SELF OR THREATENING TO DO SO:

They didn't believe me.
Don't stay away because of a measly joke.

They thought / (we were going to hold up the United Dairy Farmers).
My first wife and I didn't get along together at all.
(She says) / I'm crazy / (but I'm not).
Can't you understand / (what I'm saying)?
That doctor will never understand me.
I don't want nobody to pity me.
(They said) / I hadn't made my ideas clear.
My kids won't believe / that I'm sick.

Self threatened with death from subhuman or inanimate objects or death-dealing situation (IIb2)

(If you dream about dead people) / you'll join them in the near future.
One of the railroad cars would have hit me / (if I hadn't jumped)
There were dangerous times in my life, like World War I.
Well, I might get run over by a bus.
(Those were the days) / when death seemed very close.
(It looked) / as if the rattler was close enough to do a good job on me.
(I dreamed) / I was being strangled by a monster.
(It was the kind of auto accident) / that might easily have been the end of me.

Others (subhuman, inanimate, or situation) injuring, abandoning, robbing self, or causing suffering or anguish (IIa1)

I got caught in one of the machines there and got hurt.
The continued howling of the neighborhood animals really upset me terribly.
That treatment really made me pretty sick.
That medicine gives me a wretched feeling.
(I hope) / that treatment don't paralyze me in no way.
Her cat bit me.
What I had to go through with in that treatment is awful.
(I feel lonely) / since my dog ran away and left me.
We never know what kind of an accident / (life has in store for us).
Things like that are quite nerve wracking.
We went through a terrible storm aboard that ship.
I've had many a hard bump and knock trying to get along.
(The wind was so strong) / that I couldn't get my breath.
Anybody losing a night's sleep, they feel / like they're all in.

Denial of blame (by others) (IIb1)

(The policeman told the people at the detention home) / that I wasn't involved.
(My mother said / she knew) / it hadn't been my fault.
(I knew) / they would let me go / (when they heard the facts).

(My sister said) / she wouldn't blame me / (if I did leave him).
I was never arrested before in my life.

Verbal Sample # 1 Coded for Ambivalently Directed Hostility

Name of Subject: (Hypertensive
  Negro woman outpatient)   Interviewer:
Date: Total Words: 204
Name of Study: Correction Factor: 0.4902

Well, I want to tell you about during the war / when I went to Okla-
                                        IId3
homa to visit my husband. / I had heard / that people would pick
your pockets / if you sit in the station in St. Louis / and I finally got
                    IIa2
my ticket / but they made me wait in line a long time. / When we got
                                IIc3
to Oklahoma / that is / where the colored and white couldn't sit together on the train / and I moved to another section. / Then when
my husband met me, / he said / he had another girl friend now, /
                    IId3
and that really got me upset and everything. / He never had told
                                                    IIb1
me / he wanted to make a change / and he kept saying / it wasn't
                            IIa2
anything / I had done. / So he never came around to see me much /
while I was there, / and then the little room I had, / there were rats
                                    IIa1
in that area / and I was afraid / one might bite me / while I was
sleeping and everything. / Then after the war when he came back, /
                        IId3
he just kept running with other women and worrying me. / He would
                    IIc3
get mad at me and never come home. / So finally I put in for a divorce / and I've never been really well since.

*TABULATION OF VERBAL SAMPLE # 1 CODED FOR
AMBIVALENTLY DIRECTED HOSTILITY*

Correction Factor (C.F.) = 0.4902

Subcategory	Total weight
IId3 × 3	9
IIc3 × 2	6
IIa2 × 2	4
IIa1 × 1	1
IIb1 × 1	1
Total	21

Raw score   10.29
Corrected score (+ ½ C.F.)   10.54
Square root   3.25

THE AMBIVALENT HOSTILITY SCALE

Verbal Sample # 2 Coded for Ambivalently Directed Hostility

Name of Subject:
  (Male psychiatric inpatient)   Interviewer:
Date: Total Words: 191
Name of Study: Correction Factor: 0.5236

Uh okay, okay, yeah. / Something happened to me, yeah. / Jus . . .
                                 IIa3
something happened to me / I got my jawbone broke / and I got my
     IIa3   IId3   IId3
jawbone broke / and I got robbed. / Got robbed / and then I got
     IIa3   IId3
jawbone broken. / And I, see / and somebody robbed me. / So I stayed home Sunday. / Come out the hospital Monday. / And I come out / and I stayed out / and can't help the (3 words omitted) / So I went upstairs to the doctor / and the doctors there are mighty fine. /
              IIa1   IIa1
I had my bone broke, / see / you see, / this one is broke on this
                       IIa1
side / well this other one was broken on that side too. / But it been
    IIa1   IIa1
broke a long time ago / see. / That time my lip was split too / see. /
                                                  IIa2
I was telling this other patient about it / but seemed like / he didn't believe / anything I said to him somehow. / Seems like / he's just
               IIc3
take a dislike or something to me / I don't know why. / The others don't act that way. / I'm a contract man / see. / I'm a hod / I'm a hod-carrying laborer, union man. / I'm a union man. / I belong to the AFL-CIO. /

TABULATION OF VERBAL SAMPLE # 2 CODED FOR
AMBIVALENTLY DIRECTED HOSTILITY

Correction Factor (C.F.) = 0.5236

Subcategory	Total weight
IIa3 × 3	9
IIc3 × 1	3
IId3 × 3	9
IIa2 × 1	2
IIa1 × 5	5
Total	28

Raw score   14.66
Corrected score (+ ½ C.F.)   14.92
Square root   3.86

Verbal Sample # 3 Coded for Ambivalently Directed Hostility

Name of Subject:
   (Female psychiatric inpatient)   Interviewer:
Date: Total Words: 201
Name of Study: Correction Factor: 0.4975

I've been married one year. / The reason // why I am here // is /
                         IIb3
because last Thursday my husband jumped on me. / My mother called the police. / About fifteen minutes after that the police came. /
                       IId3
My husband had padlocked me and my little girl in the house. / He was going down the steps. / He was going off to work. / So that police told him to go back up the steps and unlock the door / because
                       IIb2
if the house would catch on fire / me and my little girl wouldn't have no way of getting out. / So he unlocked the door / and the police
                       IIb3
asked / what was going on. / I told them / that he had jumped on me. / And then I went down to city hall building to swear out a warrant to have my husband arrested. / So my husband said / he
          IIc3   IIc3
was going to have some detectives pick me up / because I was mentally ill. / When they came to get me / I asked them why / and they
                       IIc3
said / that my husband said / that I was mentally ill. / So I've been out at the hospital until September 15th. / My husband's not allowed
                       IIa2
here. / I asked the doctor why. / He said / he may upset me more. /

TABULATION OF VERBAL SAMPLE # 3 CODED FOR
AMBIVALENTLY DIRECTED HOSTILITY

Correction Factor (C.F.) = 0.4975

Subcategory	Total weight
IIb3 × 2	6
IIc3 × 3	9
IId3 × 1	3
IIa2 × 1	2
IIb2 × 1	2
Total	22

Raw score   10.94
Corrected score (+ ½ C.F.)   11.19
Square root   3.34

Verbal Sample # 4 Coded for Ambivalently Directed Hostility

Name of Subject:
   (Male medical inpatient)
Date:
Name of Study:

Interviewer:
Total Words: 196
Correction Factor: 0.5102

Well, while I've been on this ward / I've seen some doctors. / A doctor would come around to see me. / Most patients they just give 15
                                               IIa2
minutes visit every day. / They didn't give me but one. / Three weeks ago they gave me one treatment on Saturday / and then they didn't
            IIa2   IIa2
give me another one. / They ain't been, ain't been around since but
                                  IIa2
that one time. / Ain't doing nothing for me. / That's all I got, one
                                       IIa2
treatment. / And done nothing but draw some blood out of me and urinate in bottles and fill up jugs urinating. / Ain't come and see,
                                 IId3
ain't none, ain't none of them come and see me. / Could come and give me another X ray or something. / They ought to let me see /
                                                   IIa2
how far I'm gone. / You know, / they ain't telling me nothing. /
                                                              IIa2
Seems to me / like you're doing something for me. / They ain't doing
                                                         IIa2
nothing. / All those weeks and no doctors come around. / They won't
 IIa2   IIa2
do nothing. / Put me away over in a corner like this. / Poor old goat
                                                                 IId3
ain't got no money to go to the doctor with. / Just let you here to
                                     IIa2
die or something. / Ain't going to do nothing for me. /

TABULATION OF VERBAL SAMPLE # 4 CODED FOR
AMBIVALENTLY DIRECTED HOSTILITY

Correction Factor (C.F.) = 0.5102

Subcategory	Total weight
IId3 × 2	6
IIa2 × 11	22
Total	28

Raw score   14.29
Corrected score (+ ½ C.F.)   14.54
Square root   3.81

Verbal Sample # 5 Coded for Ambivalently Directed Hostility

Name of Subject:
  (Female psychiatric inpatient)
Date:
Name of Study:

Interviewer:
Total Words: 203
Correction Factor: 0.4926

The most interesting part of my life is / what's happening to me / and why my sister and them so interested in my life. / Why did they
                         II*d*3   II*d*3
want to put me away / and why they want my kids taken away from me. / And it all started / back when my mother died / and up until
                      II*a*1
now it's getting worser and worser. / And I do / all I can for my
                                    II*c*3   II*c*3
sisters and them / and they just say / I'm crazy / and they makes
                          II*d*3
fun of me / and they don't want me around them. / And so that's
                                          II*a*1
why / I guess / I started this / and it's beginning to bother me worser and worser and worser. / And I want to get away from it. / And I'm just in misery / and it seem / like I scared of something. / Then
                                                        II*c*3
just like I told you / my older sister said / I was crazy / and I need
  II*d*3   II*d*3
to be put away / and they need to take the kids away from me. / And at times when I get in these raves like this / I just want to go off / and I wants to start drinking / and at times I don't pay the kids any attention. / But I don't leave them in the house or nothing. /

TABULATION OF VERBAL SAMPLE # 5 CODED FOR AMBIVALENTLY DIRECTED HOSTILITY

Correction Factor (C.F.) = 0.4926

Subcategory	Total weight
II*c*3 × 3	9
II*d*3 × 5	15
II*a*1 × 2	2
Total	26

Raw score   12.81
Corrected score (+ ½ C.F.)   13.05
Square root   3.61

Verbal Sample # 6 Coded for Ambivalently Directed Hostility

Name of Subject:
  (Male psychiatric outpatient)
Date:
Name of Study:

Interviewer:
Total Words: 219
Correction Factor: 0.4566

My wife called / and I didn't know what to do about her. / She was
                                                    IIa2
crying / when I left. / She says / she don't know / if she loves me
                                    IId3
any more. / She don't know / if she wants to stay with me. / And she went to pieces, sitting there watching television / and all of a sudden she started crying. / Well I don't know / how much longer
          IIa1   IIa1
I can put up with it. / I don't know / how much longer I can put up with it. / I was talking to her / and then I said / do you
                        IIa2   IIa2
love me? / She said / don't ask me that, / I can't tell you that. / Started crying again. / She don't want to associate with any of my
              IIc3   IIc3
relatives / and her family don't like me. / So we had an argument or two about that. / And I started noticing right after our last talk /
                                                    IIa2
that she was // I guess / you would say // avoiding me. / Every time
                        IIa2
I'd get around her / she'd try to be some place else. / If I'd go put
                                                    IIa2
my arms around her or something / she would turn away. / I don't know / just what it is myself. / She don't go no place. / Been sitting there in that house for two-and-a-half, three weeks. / I try to get her out on the weekends or something / if I ain't working. /

TABULATION OF VERBAL SAMPLE # 6 CODED FOR AMBIVALENTLY DIRECTED HOSTILITY

Correction Factor (C.F.) = 0.4566

Subcategory	Total weight
IIc3 × 2	6
IId3 × 1	3
IIa2 × 6	12
IIa1 × 2	2
Total	23

Raw score	10.50
Corrected score (+ ½ C.F.)	10.73
Square root	3.28

CHAPTER X
The Social Alienation–Personal Disorganization (Schizophrenic) Scale

INTRODUCTION

As with the four affect scales presented in the earlier sections of this manual, this content analysis method for measuring the severity of personal disorganization and social alienation can be applied to verbal communications obtained in a variety of ways. Most of our own use of this scale has involved its application to the content analysis of verbal samples obtained by standardized procedures (see p. 5). The tape-recorded speech is transcribed, and each clause is examined and coded according to the appropriate category. As described in our validation studies (Gottschalk and Gleser, 1969), this scale can discriminate the relative severity of the schizophrenic syndrome and can also be used to discriminate schizophrenic from nonschizophrenic individuals (Gottschalk and Gleser, 1964).

This section contains the following materials related to the use of the Social Alienation–Personal Disorganization Scale:

1. The several pages of categories and scoring symbols of the scale are presented together with the weights assigned to each category (Schedule 5). Verbal items found to signify evidence of social alienation or personal disorganization are given positive weights, and items associated with more healthy, nonschizophrenic behavior are given negative weights. Items which make no consistent contribution to the prediction of criterion scores are assigned zero weights. We continue to score these unweighted content items, however, because we have noted that when a category is dropped from the scale and no longer kept in the scoring system, there is a tendency for scorers to interpret statements which would normally have been scored in such a category as scorable in closely allied categories. The maintenance of the unweighted cate-

gories in the scale thus tends to maintain differentiation and in the long run to preserve scoring reliability. For example, the category of references to others as bad, dangerous, having low value or worth, being strange, ill or malfunctioning (category ID1) is given a zero weight. If it were eliminated from the scale, there would be a tendency to place statements properly codable in this category into a closely allied category, such as self unfriendly to others, category IB1).

The scale contains five major groupings of categories: I. Interpersonal references; II. Intrapersonal references; III. References to disorganization and repetition; IV. Questions or other references directed to the interviewer; V. References to religious or biblical topics.

2. Following a description of the Social Alienation–Personal Disorganization Scale (Schedule 5), the rules for use in scoring the various categories are provided.

3. An extensive list of examples of coded clauses for the various categories and subcategories is given. Where necessary, in order to understand the context in which the clause was assigned a particular code, the context is supplied but is set off in parentheses.

4. Following the examples for each category of the Social Alienation–Personal Disorganization Scale, there will be found several coded verbal samples and a suggested method of tabulating the results.

SCHEDULE 5
Social Alienation and Personal Disorganization (Schizophrenic) Scale*

Weights	Content Categories and Scoring Symbols
	I. Interpersonal references (including fauna and flora).
	A. To thoughts, feelings or reported actions of avoiding, leaving, deserting, spurning, not understanding of others.
0	1. Self avoiding others.
+1	2. Others avoiding self.
	B. To unfriendly, hostile, destructive thoughts, feelings, or actions.
+1	1. Self unfriendly to others.
+⅓	2. Others unfriendly to self.
	C. To congenial and constructive thoughts, feelings or actions.
−2	1. Others helping, being friendly toward others.
−2	2. Self helping, being friendly toward others.
−2	3. Others helping, being friendly toward self.

130   THE "SCHIZOPHRENIC" SCALE

Schedule 5 (*contd.*)

Weights   Content Categories and Scoring Symbols

           D. To others.
0   1. Being bad, dangerous, strange, ill, malfunctioning, having low value or worth.
−1   2. Being intact, satisfied, healthy, well.

     II. Intrapersonal references.

+2   A. To disorientation—references indicating disorientation for time, place, person, or other distortion of reality—past, present, or future (do not score more than one item per clause under this category).

          B. To self.
            1*a*. Physical illness, malfunctioning (references to illness or
0   symptoms due primarily to cellular or tissue damage).
            1*b*. Psychological malfunctioning (references to illness or
+1   symptoms due primarily to emotions or psychological reactions *not secondary* to cellular or tissue damage).
            1*c*. Malfunctioning of indeterminate origin (references to ill-
0   ness or symptoms not definitely attributable either to emotions or cellular damage).
−2   2. Getting better.
−1   3*a*. Intact, satisfied, healthy, well; definite positive affect or valence indicated.
−1   3*b*. Intact, satisfied, healthy, well; flat, factual or neutral attitudes expressed.
+½   4. Not being prepared or able to produce, perform, act, not knowing, not sure.
            5. To being controlled, feeling controlled, wanting control,
+½   asking for control or permission, being obliged or having to do, think, or experience something.

+3   C. Denial of feelings, attitudes, or mental state of the self.

          D. To food.
0   1. Bad, dangerous, unpleasant, or otherwise negative; interferences or delays in eating; too much and wish to have less; too little and wish to have more.
0   2. Good or neutral.

          E. To weather.
−1   1. Bad, dangerous, unpleasant, or otherwise negative (not sunny, not clear, uncomfortable, etc.).
−1   2. Good, pleasant, or neutral.

          F. To sleep.
0   1. Bad, dangerous, unpleasant, or otherwise negative, too much, too little.
0   2. Good, pleasant, or neutral.

     III. Disorganization and repetition.

          A. Signs of disorganization.
+1   1. Remarks or words that are not understandable or inaudible.
0   2. Incomplete sentences, clauses, phrases; blocking.
+2   3. Obviously erroneous or fallacious remarks or conclusions; illogical or bizarre statements.

Schedule 5 (*contd.*)

Weights	Content Categories and Scoring Symbols
	B. Repetition of ideas in sequence.
0	1. Words separated only by a word (excluding instances due to grammatical and syntactical convention, where words are repeated, e.g., "as far as," "by and by," and so forth; also excluding instances where such words as "I" and "the" are separated by a word).
+1	2. Phrases or clauses (separated only by a phrase or a clause).
	IV. References to the interviewer.
+1	A. Questions directed to the interviewer.
+½	B. Other references to the interviewer.
+1	V. Religious and biblical references.

* The weights given in this table are those we now use. The original weights used for this scale are described in our 1958 publication (see also Gottschalk and Gleser, 1969). It was thought that these original weights might be more sensitive in longitudinal studies. It should be noted that in this earlier study, categories signifying evidence of the schizophrenic syndrome were given negative weights, whereas currently, such items are given positive weights.

It is possible that the original (non-zero) weightings might result in more accurate discrimination whenever repetitive measures of severity of the schizophrenic syndrome are to be made. A discussion of these weights may be found in Gottschalk *et al.*, 1961; Gottschalk and Gleser, 1969.

RULES FOR SCORING CATEGORIES [1]

1. While the unit of verbal communication to be scored is the grammatical clause, it should be noted that, due to the sometimes fragmented or incoherent nature of schizophrenic speech, we have exercised somewhat greater flexibility in interpreting the grammatical clause on verbal samples scored with this measure.

2. While, in general, references to the subcategories of this scale are scored regardless of the tense in which they are verbalized, important exceptions to this rule regarding tense are categories IIB2 and IIB3*a* and IIB3*b*, that is, "getting better" and "feeling well." These categories are not scored when they are in a conditional tense or in the form of a wish.

3. Use literal more than inferential criteria when deciding whether or not to code a category. This means that the principal criterion as to whether a category is to be scored depends on what the subject actually says in a clause and not so much on what the scorer tends to infer. If a repeated idea is inferable in a series

---

[1] See also general rules applicable to all scales, p. 23.

of clauses but is not definitely restated, the item is not to be rescored.

4. Except where otherwise noted, several different categories may be tallied per clause. For example, "we" and "us" can be coded in two different categories, self and others, as both categories are applicable. Avoid, however, consistent overscoring. Thus, if a clause is tallied as not being understandable or vague or bizarre (category IIIA), it is not generally likely to be scorable also in a category that requires the communication of some definite bits of information. It is recognized, however, that there are exceptions to this point. With some frequency, clauses occur which may be coded for incomplete sentences, clauses, phrases, blocking (IIIA2) and for repetition of either words (IIIB1) or clauses and phrases (IIIB2). In this instance, we have followed the procedure of assigning only one score and of giving precedence to coding indicating repetition, that is, either IIIB1 or IIIB2 rather than IIIA2.

5. Where a series of content references are made in a clause, the category is to be scored only once instead of the total number of references. For example, when the subject lists the food items he ate for a meal in a series fashion, the food category (IID) is to be tallied only once.

6. References that fall into any one of the designated categories but involve infrahuman animals or inanimate objects may be scored the same as if they were about humans.

EXAMPLES OF SOCIAL ALIENATION–PERSONAL DISORGANIZATION

Interpersonal References (I)

Four major categories of interpersonal relations are scored: A. Avoidance-type relationships; B. Unfriendly, hostile, or destructive kinds of behavior, including thoughts and feelings as well as overt behavior; C. Congenial, constructive, or friendly kinds of interpersonal relations; and D. References to others as bad or malfunctioning or as good or well-functioning.

The first three types of references, that is, categories A, B, and C, specify the initiator of the action and the directions. The fourth category, D, differs in that specification of the actor is not required. All interpersonal references (A, B, C, and D) may be scored for fauna, flora, and inanimate objects as well as for human interaction.

AVOIDANCE IN INTERPERSONAL RELATIONS (IA)

While avoidance in interpersonal relations might in some instances be subsumed under unfriendly behavior (category IB), we have chosen to separate it from other forms of hostile or destructive behavior. Thus, a statement like "I left the room / whenever he came in" may also imply hostility but is more clearly indicative of avoidance behavior and is so scored.

Avoidance behavior is scored even when the material to be coded is verbalized in such a way that one feels there might have been no alternative to the act of avoidance. For example, the statement of a hospitalized patient "I have six children / whom I've been away from for three years" is considered a scorable clause in the category of avoidance in interpersonal relations (category IA1).

We include as types of avoidance behavior leaving, deserting, spurning and not understanding. Examples of each of these are given below, although the separate categories of avoidance are obviously not discrete and there is much overlapping.

By Self (IA1)

SELF AVOIDING OTHERS:

I don't want to talk with you. (IA1 and IVB)
I wouldn't date anyone / (when I was young).
I don't like to go out and meet people.
I made myself sick just sitting at home and not doing anything.
I wouldn't want my mother to be back alive again.
I used to stay in the house pretty much at times.
I had that trouble with a rocking chair / and I run off one time.
  (IIB1*b* and IA1)
I got a room by myself.
If I had never met him / (my life would have been entirely different).

SELF LEAVING OR DESERTING OTHERS:

I broke up with this boy.
I have to get the divorce.
I have six children / whom I've been away from for three years.
Can I go now, doctor? (IVA and IA1)
I've been trying to get out of here since Christmas.

(I wish) / they'd let me out of here.
I quit my job.
I left school after one year there.
I got a divorce that year.
I left the job on a leave of absence.
(I'm almost sorry) / that I left there. (IIB1b and IA1)
(I wouldn't mind re-enlisting) / if I was out of here. (IIC and IA1)

SELF SPURNING OTHERS:

I got rid of my old car.
I like them to leave me alone.
(I didn't like the job) / so I didn't take it.
I'm not going to talk to him.

SELF NOT UNDERSTANDING OTHERS:

Sometimes I can't understand him.
I don't know / (what you're talking about). (IIB4, IA1, IVB)
She doesn't make sense to me.
I didn't seem to have any idea what it was about.
It wasn't very clear / (what they meant).
I couldn't seem to hear him ever.

By Others (IA2)

OTHERS AVOIDING SELF:

She didn't want to go hunting with me.
(My brother said) / he would pay for the glasses / and he ain't been
   here since then. (IC3 and IA2)
He forgot to pick me up this morning.
They will always more or less ignore me.
I don't have any friends.
He is going to take the baby away from me.
(I asked him to write) / but I never heard from him yet.
My family ought to come more than once a year.
(They come out on Xmas) / but they don't come the rest of the year.
   (IC3 and IA2)
They don't want an extra person in their house.
I can't seem to get acquainted with the girls real well in this ward.

OTHERS LEAVING OR DESERTING SELF:

My wife divorced me.
I been losing friends because of these voices. (IA1 and IIIA3a)
I never have any visitors.
My people never visit me.
He was going to get a divorce from me.
I'll miss you / when you go away. (IIB1b, IVB, and IA2)

He had me put out in a sanitarium.
They just stuck me away here in the state hospital.

OTHERS SPURNING SELF:

The factory laid me off.
They don't want me in their home.
None of the boys will date me.
None of my relatives would sign me out.
(Alfie said) / he didn't want me any more.
They wouldn't tell me / (what it was about).
I never heard from him again.

OTHERS NOT UNDERSTANDING SELF:

They didn't always understand everything either.
Don't you know / what I'm saying? (IA2 and IVA)
He just didn't see things / the way I did.

REFERENCES TO UNFRIENDLY, HOSTILE, OR DESTRUCTIVE THOUGHTS, FEELINGS, OR ACTIONS (IB)

As with the category (IA) designating messages communicating avoidance behavior or feelings, this content category is subdivided according to whether the behavior is initiated by the self and directed toward others or initiated by others and directed toward the self. Unfriendly behavior that is primarily an avoidance of the self or others is scored under the classification of avoidance (IA). When the subject of the clause is the self and the nonself (we, our), the clause is coded as the self unfriendly to others (IB1). Similarly, when the object of the unfriendly or hostile behavior is the self and others, the clause is classified others unfriendly to the self (IB2). Unfriendly or destructive and hostile behavior may vary from verbal to physical and may be real or imagined; it may involve humans or infrahumans, that is, flora, fauna, or inanimate objects.

Self unfriendly, hostile, destructive in interpersonal relation with others (IB1)

ACTIONS INVOLVING HUMANS:

I would like to start a fight with him.
I stuck a Buick dealer with our old car.
I've been incriminating against my friends. (IB1 and IIIA1)
(He was the boy) / I was supposed to fight.
(Those are the people) / I don't care for much.

I was fighting everyone.
I never got along with the other pupils too well.
I beat the daylights out of him.
My buddy and I were throwing rotten oranges at the little kids.
We had just one little disagreement. (IB1 and IB2)
I always argued with him about it.
I don't like anybody to bother me. (IB1 and IB2)

ACTIONS INVOLVING INFRAHUMANS, INANIMATE OBJECTS, OR SITUATIONS:

I don't especially like this place.
I had to live in a room with my father / which I didn't like. (IIB5 and IB1)
I tried to steal some apples from the yard.
I hate those old chairs.
We shot our bombers over the air fields.
I was going to tear the windows out.
I ripped the blouse to shreds.
I kicked the dog down the steps.

Others unfriendly, hostile, or destructive to the self (IB2)

HUMANS UNFRIENDLY TO SELF:

My brother pushed me off the chair.
She hates me.
She thinks / I'm an awful thing.
(I don't know) / if they'll give me my false teeth or not. (IIB4, IC3, and IB2)
She always causes trouble to me.
You look real stern sitting there. (IVB and IB2)
Four men came to take me to court.
They usually punish me for smoking.
The tenants didn't give me any rent for a whole year.
I don't see / why they're keeping me here. (IIB4 and IB2)
Someone opened the door and knocked my teeth out.
They didn't like me very much.
She made me her prime target for her temper outbursts.
They don't care for me any more.
I got the whipping of my life.
She took my rosary away from me.
He degraded me in front of the eyes of the other students.
She was going to beat me up.
Her temper was directed at me.
We got in a fight or something. (IB1 and IB2, because the self could be both subject and object of the hostility.)
I've told you / most of what they've done to me out here. (IVB and IB2)

They hurt me in this hospital.
(The guy saw me) / and he threw a rock at me.
He took my job away from me.
He cut me with a glass.

INFRAHUMAN OR INANIMATE OBJECTS UNFRIENDLY TO THE SELF:

The dog nipped me in the heel.
The limb scratched my right shoulder.
The poison gas from the gas drill left me like this.
Even their cat didn't like me.
The bull started chasing us.
We were all stung by bees that time.

CONGENIAL AND CONSTRUCTIVE THOUGHTS, ACTIONS,
OR FEELINGS (IC)

This interpersonal category has three subcategories involving behavior of (1) others to others, (2) self to others, and (3) others to self. This category may be thought of as the antithesis of the type of interpersonal relations which are hostile and destructive (coded IB). These interactions (IC) involve friendly acts, helpfulness, sympathetic treatment, kindness, and warm interpersonal behavior. The range of friendly acts which are codable includes generally friendly greetings as well as gifts or substantial aid and comfort. Constructive behavior may involve interaction with subhumans or situational factors as well as interrelationships with human beings. It is especially easy to overcode in this category, since a multiple subject and multiple object can lead to the interpretation that all three subcategories should be scored. We have followed a rule of never giving more than two scores per clause and of usually assigning only one. Whether two scores are assigned depends in part on the extent to which the context focuses on the self only or on the self and others. Two scores are not assigned when the others are somewhat shadowy, distant, or generalized as opposed to specifically mentioned characters in the subject's narration.

Others helping, being friendly toward others (IC1)

We're looking forward to seeing them. (IC1 and IC2)
He really liked the Army.
The fig wasp pollinates the fig.
They worked together for 20 years or more.
He liked going out to welcome the planes.

138 THE "SCHIZOPHRENIC" SCALE

The doctor helped him get a job.
They prepared us for the task. (ICl and IC3)
He got the car ready for them.
They gave us something to take home. (IC1 and IC3)
She used to help my mother with the cooking and cleaning.
She is going to get married this year.
She took good care of her sick father.
The Ladies Aid brings us treats every third week. (IC1 and IC3)
He has someone to take care of him.
They enjoyed seeing the children.
Something worthwhile would really make him happy.
They took a bus load of kids from the orphanage to the ball game.
God's love inspires them. (IC1 and V)
The dog never left his side.
They were drawn in fellowship with Jesus Christ. (ICI and V)

Self helping, being friendly to others (IC2)

I was always very sociable.
I got married last summer.
I help out on the wards.
I want to help with her spring house cleaning.
In some cases, I can console them.
We used to be real friendly. (IC2 and IC3)
I always say hello to her / (when I go in).
I'd like for him to be my friend.
I enjoyed the visit with my mother.
Me and my brother go to movies together all the time. (IC2 and IC3)
I was very close to my daughter.
I get along just fine with the nurses here.
I made an apron for my mother.
I like my doctor.
I usually talk to the people at the bus stop.
O God, we thank Thee for the hope of a better world. (IC2 and V)
I fed the fish every day.
I thank God for the beautiful day. (IC2, IIE2 and V)
We kept the bird / until it was well enough to fly. (IC2 and ID2)
(Did you get the magazine) / I put on your table this morning? (IC2 and IVB)
I was thrilled to be with him.
I like to weed the flower beds and keep them nice.
I gave her a birthday present.
I hate to see you leave. (IC2, IVB, and IIB1*b*)

Others helping, being friendly toward the self (IC3)

(I hope) / you will forgive me.
She gave me a reference / (when I left).
That car really got me all over the country.

THE "SCHIZOPHRENIC" SCALE

I used to have lots of visitors.
Mom came to see me last Wednesday.
Will you help me go home? (IVA and IC3)
Talking with people helps me out a lot.
The medicine really gave me relief.
The flowers // they sent // were pretty.
Then they gave me treatments. (IC3 and IIb1b)
They put me on some kind of medication.
They were very friendly.
I had a lot of friends.
They contributed to my upkeep.
He brought me a vase of flowers.
I got something else for Christmas.
Maybe this will help me in some way. (That is, this five-minute verbal sample.)
For my birthday I got two slips and some money from my daughter's husband.
He's always been real nice to me.
(I wish) / you would put in for a pass for me. (IVB and IC3)
(He asked me) / if I would marry him.
You've always listened to me. (IVB and IC3)
They sure were good to me in that foster home.
He was going to pay for my glasses.
My sister helped me for a while.
God will take care of me. (IC3 and V)
The kitten would sit in my lap and purr.
(I dreamed) / my mother was coming to get me.
The bus ride was good for me.

INTERPERSONAL REFERENCES TO OTHERS AS: (1) BEING BAD, DANGEROUS, STRANGE, ILL, MALFUNCTIONING, HAVING LOW VALUE OR WORTH. (2) BEING INTACT, SATISFIED, HEALTHY, GOOD, WELL (ID)

Interpersonal references scored in the ID category may involve good or bad qualities or actions of people, subhumans, situations, or inanimate objects. The avoidance or destructive behaviors of others to others are scored here rather than in the IA and IB content categories discussed above.

Others (including fauna, flora, things, places) being bad, dangerous, strange, ill, malfunctioning, having low value or worth (ID1)

People didn't know what to do.
One fellow fell off the roof.
My mother is in the hospital.
He died.

Mary caused them a lot of trouble.
Another fellow from there disappeared recently.
There was such an uproar over it.
We were stung badly. (ID1 and IIB1*a*)
It was just a mishap for anybody.
We had an accident. (ID1 and IIB1*a*)
She had a heart attack.
His car turned over on the driver's side.
They put her in a room by herself; / they said / that she was a bad girl. (Two scores for ID1.)
They had quite a few bad things happen to them.
He met with foul play, according to the newspapers.
It sounded like a dog growling.
They were both fired.
He got a hacking cough while there.
I didn't go to the funeral.
In my dreams I could see his grave.
Their father deserted them.
The flowers had wilted.
He shot the deer.
We have to suffer through things like that. (ID1 and IIB1*b*)
The windshield was smashed to smithereens.
It was a poor home to go to.
The glare from the headlights was awful.
The room was dirty.
It was only a cheap dress anyway.
Things could be a whole lot worse at home.
She was behaving peculiarly.
They are too old to go somewhere else.
The car wouldn't work any more.
The plane had a burnt-out motor.

Others (including fauna, flora, things, places) intact, satisfied, healthy, well (ID2)

Everything turned out all right for her.
He was a really good roofer.
Betty has a job now.
My folks are all good people.
Everything was going just fine.
My sister works every day.
He was promoted to boss.
The mountains there are very picturesque.
It was the best running car.
The spectacles // I have // are fine.
Ruth had a beautiful baby.
The azaleas were beautiful that year.
You have a nice office. (IVB and ID2)

They had wonderful herds of Angus cattle.
My daughter's house is so pretty.
Atlantic City was really great.
We enjoyed the movie. (ID2 and IIB3a)
He had a good vacation last month.
His doctor knows / his job well.

Intrapersonal References (II)

References scored in the intrapersonal category are those which deal primarily with the state of the speaker with reference to a wide range of feelings, thoughts, activities, or behaviors: A. Disorientation as to time, place, or person; B. Physical, psychological, indeterminate malfunctioning or healthy functioning; C. A denial of some state or behavior of the self; D. References to food; E. Weather; F. Sleep.

REFERENCES INDICATING DISORIENTATION FOR TIME, PLACE, OR PERSON, OR OTHER DISTORTION OF REALITY (IIA)

As noted in Schedule 5, references indicative of disorientation of any kind may be coded whether they are verbalized in the past, present, or future tenses. If a clause indicates disorientation for more than one modality, that is, for person and time or place and person, such content is scored only once. By and large, a clause scored for disorientation is not also given a score for other information. For example, the statement "I like being here at this hotel" (patient is in a state hospital) is scored only as revealing disorientation (IIA), it is not also scored for the self being satisfied (IIB3a).

> I saw my husband for the first time, for the second time, no, well for the some time in three years.
> I'm very glad to recognize Sunday sometimes.
> I worked there in 1937, / about a year ago, I guess. (It is 1956 at time of verbal sample.)
> I'd like to know / what I'm in here for. (Speaker is in state mental hospital.)
> She's about two or three years old now and / I haven't seen her for three or four years.
> Are you the chief inspector? (The interviewer had explained who he was and the purpose of verbal sample.)
> There's a station next to General Hospital. (There is no station located there.)
> I saw an accident in the hospital church yard.
> He brought me a little box child.

Here in San Antonio. . . . (Speaker is in Cincinnati.)
(I didn't remember meeting them the time before) / and I couldn't remember anything then for seven months.
That tranquilizer made me to where / I couldn't remember anything. (IIB5 and IIA)
I don't know what this place is—a police station?
Hello Mother. / How are you? / I'll see you pretty soon, mom. (Patient is in state mental hospital, speaking to male doctor. Each clause is coded IIA.)
There isn't much information for me to say, Father. (Person is speaking to a doctor.)
I've been here a year now. (Record shows patient has been in hospital for 17 years.)
Father hasn't told me my age / (but he said) / that I'm 99 billion times another number age. (IIA and IIIA3)

REFERENCES TO THE SELF AS MALFUNCTIONING, GETTING BETTER, OR WELL-FUNCTIONING (IIB)

References to any type of malfunctioning of the self (IIB1)

References in this intrapersonal category are all coded IIB1 and then further categorized as to type of malfunctioning: (*a*) physical illness or references to symptoms or illness due primarily to cellular or tissue damage; (*b*) psychological malfunctioning, including all references to illness or symptoms which are due primarily to feelings, emotion, or other psychological reactions *not* secondary to cellular or tissue damage; and (*c*) malfunctioning of the self of an indeterminate origin or nature, that is, references to symptoms or illness which cannot clearly be attributed to either psychological or physiological factors.

In discriminating between these three subcategories, it is especially important that the context in which a codable clause is embedded, be taken into account. Such factors as age or diagnosis may aid the coder in deciding how a clause is to be coded. For example, a verbal sample from a hospitalized patient with terminal cancer containing references to various organic aches and pains may be coded in the physical malfunctioning (IIB1*a*) category unless the patient otherwise specifies; whereas, the same types of references from a psychiatric patient more likely fall within the classification of malfunctioning of indeterminate origin (IIB1*c*).

References to psychological malfunctioning cover a wide range of feelings and emotions. While they are all included in the IIB1*b* category, we have broken down such references into subtypes and provided examples of each. The subcategories include: (1) References to feelings of deprivation or rejection or desertion; this category should not be confused with the content category others avoiding the self (IA2), where the focus is on interpersonal relations rather than upon an intrapsychic state of the speaker. (2) References to feelings of inadequacy, low value, or worthlessness. (3) References to feelings of strangeness, estrangement, or loss of identity or dissociation. (4) Reference to other feelings or psychological symptoms or illness.

When the references to actual or threatened malfunctioning includes the self and others, as in the clause "We had an accident on our vacation," two scores are given: physical malfunctioning of the self (IIB1a) and malfunctioning of others (ID1).

REFERENCES TO ILLNESSES OR SYMPTOMS DUE PRIMARILY TO CELLULAR OR TISSUE DAMAGE (IIB1a)

Those gallstones cause trouble.
I've been operated on a couple of times.
I suffered from loss of weight, colds, coughs, and night sweats.
All my teeth were pulled.
Old age makes me get tired. (IIB1a and IIB5)
I still have a scar on my kneecap.
I was wounded at that time.
I have a sore on the inside of my mouth.
I broke my arm.
I had spinal meningitis.
We had an accident. (IIB1a and ID1)
(He said) / I had psoriasis.
Our car turned over on the driver's side. (IIB1a and ID1)
My eyesight is nearly gone.
We were stung badly. (IIB1a and ID1)

PSYCHOLOGICAL MALFUNCTIONING.—REFERENCES TO ILLNESS OR SYMPTOMS DUE PRIMARILY TO EMOTIONS OR PSYCHOLOGICAL REACTIONS AND NOT SECONDARY TO CELLULAR OR TISSUE DAMAGE (IIB1b)

References to feelings of deprivation or rejection or desertion:

I want to get out so bad.
I miss New York now.
I haven't got a mother, father, or anything.
I'm out of work again.
I saw my husband Sunday for the first time in three years.
I don't have any living children.
With such short passes, I don't get a chance to hunt for a job.

We were pinching pennies in those days.
I don't have much enjoyment in life.
Then I fell off a roof.
I am lonesome.
I don't have anyone to sign me out of the hospital.
(My people live in a trailer) / and there ain't no room for me.
We couldn't get our vacation this summer. (IIB1b and ID1)
There wouldn't be nobody at home to stay with me.
I wish / I could have more out of life.
I've been waiting over a year to get my false teeth.
I really miss my mother.
I was considered too young for the job.
I didn't get any letter again today.
I haven't anything in the world.
(I don't see) / why I can't go home.
My home is all broken up.

References to feelings of inadequacy, low value, or worthlessness:

I only got to the seventh grade.
I'm not well enough to even keep my own house.
(I thought) / I was too light for the Army.
I'm not talented in anything very much.
It was embarrassing for me.
I've never been much to look at.
(My husband told me) / I was never going to be better / (as far as he was concerned).
Usually I talk too much.
I'm not bright enough to do that.
I wasn't a very good student.
I'm too timid for one thing.
They made me feel inferior.
I've never done anything very important in my life.
I'm sorry about doing that.
I have nothing worthy of talking about.
I did something wrong.
My life hasn't been very interesting.
I've been acting like a child.
I'm not attractive or pretty.

References to feelings of strangeness or estrangement or loss of identity or dissociation:

It was bewildering.
I never felt / I was part of the class.
I feel funny doing this.
It was so strange.
It was hard to get used to the town.
I want to die in Longview Mental Hospital.

THE "SCHIZOPHRENIC" SCALE   145

In that church I still felt strange.
I just walked in strange.
I feel / my mind is touched.
I'm losing my mind.
I'd be crazy / if I talked to him. (IIB1*b* and IA1)

References to other feelings or psychological symptoms or illness:

Things like that worry me and get on my nerves.
It's no fun being away from my children.
Little things bother me.
I don't like to wait forever to see my children again.
(That was) / where I slipped up.
I'm a psychiatric patient here.
It was really an unhappy experience.
I was frightened.
I had that trouble with a rocking chair.
I find it hard to talk over tape recorders.
I'm afraid of ending up in another state mental hospital.
Five minutes seems long.
I just sat with nothing to do.
I wasn't doing well in school.
The idea of that really hurt me.
I don't have any clock to watch.
Doing nothing drove me crazy.
I'm a little excited.
I've spent so many years here in the state mental hospital.
I couldn't afford to take a rest.
I had many hardships in those years.
I won't be so nervous then.
Lots of times we go through lots of suffering like that. (IIB1*b* and ID1)
I came here in a police car.
I wasn't much interested in doing anything.
I could tell you about an unhappy experience.
The Lord is guiding me through my trouble. (IC3, IIB1*b*, and V)
It's hard to talk for five minutes.
It scared me.
I was a troublemaker.
I'm awful helpless.
I had a lot of trouble in my life.

MALFUNCTIONING OF INDETERMINATE ORIGIN; REFERENCES TO ILLNESSES OR SYMPTOMS NOT DEFINITELY ATTRIBUTABLE EITHER TO EMOTIONS OR CELLULAR DAMAGE (IIB1*c*)

My stomach gets to kicking up.
Something is fermenting in my ear.
My bowels haven't been moving.

My health began to fail last year.
I get tired easy.
My lips are always real dry.
I don't have a lot of pep.
My back gets real weak.
I'm at General Hospital.
I was rundown and sort of underweight.
I have been here a long time. (At a general hospital.)
I wasn't well enough to handle the job.
We were quite tired.
My hands are cold.
There's something wrong with me.
I'm going to need new spectacles.
I can't stand up on my feet.
I had a bad place in my spine.
I can't hold my eyes open all the way.
I must not feel all right.
I had a convulsive spell.
I don't hear a thing.
My throat is bothering me.
I blacked out.
I take my medicine every day.

References to the self getting better (IIB2)

IIB2 is scored only in the present or past tense. Hopes and wishes for improvement or clauses expressed in future or conditional tenses are not coded. For example, "I feel better today" is coded as IIB2, but "I might feel better tomorrow" is not scored. "Getting better" may refer either to physiological or psychological functioning.

In the examples below, there are several references involving the self being helped. These are coded as getting better (IIB2) rather than as others helping the self (IC3) because from the context the subject is vague and indefinite and intrapsychic factors seem to be emphasized rather than interpersonal factors.

There is also a reference, "After the treatment, I was able to work," which one might wish to classify in the category of self well and functioning (IIB3*b*). We have preferred to score this clause as self getting better (IIB2) because it implies a comparison with former malfunctioning, and, in the context of previous inability to work, the getting better code (IIB2) appears to be a better fit than the IIB3*b* classification.

I feel much better now.
I don't have so much in my mind / (as I used to have). (IIB2 and IIB1*b*)
That helps me out.
I could sit in a chair better.
I get more strength from doing it.
I began to be interested in music again / (after not being interested in much of anything). (IIB2 and IIB1*b*)
(I know) / I'm improving every day.
(I think) / I could do that job now.
I understand a lot / (since I've been in the hospital).
It has helped me to go back to work.
That helped us along.
After the treatments, I was able to work.
I seem to be getting well.
It's better for me to keep partly busy.
I had more interests and a happier life / (than I do here). (IIB2 and IIB1*b*)
It took me a long time to get over this.
I just began to feel a little better.
(I wasn't able to do anything), / but after the treatment, I was able to cook.

References to the self as an intact, healthy, satisfied, or well person (IIB3)

This category is broken down into two subcategories indicative of the degree or intensity of the quality of well-being. Clauses indicating greater intensity or positive affect are coded IIB3*a*, and those clauses composed of rather flat, factual statements regarding activities and behavior are coded IIB3*b*. That is, one is distinguishing between "I went to work today" (coded IIB3*b*) and "I enjoyed going to work today" (coded IIB3*a*). As can be seen from Schedule 5, the same weight is given to both kinds of references. They are separated, however, in order to explore whether these references might better be differentiated after further studies.

As is the case with IIB2 above, the content categories IIB3*a* and IIB3*b* are scored only when the present or past tense occurs and not for wishes and hopes or when conditional or future tenses are used.

REFERENCES TO SELF AS INTACT, SATISFIED, HEALTHY, WELL WITH POSITIVE AFFECT (IIB3*a*)

We liked to play badminton. (IIB3*a* and ID2)
I used to be pretty good at tennis.

I made a hit with that cake.
I'm interested in some of the TV programs.
I'm right happy here.
(He showed me something) / I liked.
I enjoy picnics and going swimming.
It was exciting to be learning things.
I like to watch ball games on TV.
It was the funniest thing / (I ever saw).
I have a good time / (when I go home).
I like to get dressed up.
Most of the time I enjoy myself.
My skin disorder healed beautifully.
(I feel) / I have really accomplished something.
I have fun playing checkers and pool.
My work was always absorbing.
Everything is going fine for me.
I'm glad / (spring has come). (IIB3a and IIE2)

REFERENCES TO SELF AS INTACT, SATISFIED, HEALTHY, WELL WITH NEUTRAL AFFECT (IIB3b)

I was on the stage at that time.
I sang with the Philharmonic Chorus.
It worked for about eight weeks for me.
I did calisthenics with them.
I worked in the main kitchen and dining room.
I knew my occupation.
I worked about five places here.
In the mornings I work in the Red Cross room.
I work hard.
It makes me have good exercise.
I became a teacher then.
I'm getting along all right.
I play the piano sometimes.

Reference to the self being unprepared or unable to produce, perform or act, not knowing, not sure (IIB4)

The most frequent as well as the most clear-cut examples of this category are contained in references to not knowing what to say or what to talk about. As can be seen from the examples of clauses coded in this content category (IIB4), other references to difficulties in performing or producing may be somewhat more vague or may be verbalized as questions.

That's about all / I've got to say.
I can't sit on hard chairs with straight backs.
I don't guess / I know anything else to answer.

I don't think / I can talk five minutes.
I forget the address just now.
(I tried to get home) / but I didn't succeed.
I don't know what to say.
I can't remember / (how I came in here).
I had no prior knowledge / (of what this concerns).
I can't read without my specs.
It's hard to talk for five minutes.
You can't find a place to park.
I'm not able to work today.
I don't recall the number on that street.
I probably didn't know the answer anyway.
I can't go up steep steps any more.
That's about all / I know.
I couldn't seem to realize / (that it happened).
I don't know where to start.
I wouldn't know how to carry on a good conversation by myself.
What am I going to say?
I don't know / (why it happened that way).
I can't talk by myself this way.
I won't know for sure until tomorrow.
I can't understand about it.
I guess / I forgot to tell them about it.

References to self being controlled, feeling controlled, wanting control, asking for control or permission, being obliged to do, think, or experience something (IIB5)

The sense of control may be a reference to a realistic factor in the environment as when one is required to obey institutional rules. Or it may be a reference to seeking for controls within the self or projecting the control to other beings, human or supernatural. Frequently, questions directed to the interviewer (IVA) are also references to seeking control or permission and are therefore also scored IIB5.

Would it be okay / if I smoked? (IIB5 and IVA)
Is this the way / you want me to do things? (IIB5 and IVA)
Someday I've got to face myself.
(I knew) / the work had to be done.
I'll have to learn to be patient.
I had to know / (who would pay for the glasses).
We have to make the beds just right.
I was told to report here.
I have to get along with them / (they tell me).
I had to pay $150 to repair it.
I couldn't do it / as I should. (IIB4 and IIB5)

We have to take our trip in the fall this year.
God told me what to do. (V and IIB5)
When can I go home? (IIB5 and IVA)
They wouldn't let me go.
Could my wife bring the baby along if possible? (IIB5 and IVA)
What am I supposed to talk about? (IIB5 and IVA)
How long do I have to be here? (IIB5 and IVA)
I have to be working all the time.
(I want them to *send me home*) / and they don't *send me home*. (IIB5 and IIIB2)
We're supposed to have lunch in the cafeteria. (IIB5 and IID2)
That recollection makes me face life.
You didn't want me to behave like that. (IVB and IIB5)
(They couldn't feed themselves) / and I had to feed them. (ID1 for the first clause and IIB5 for the second.)
We have to serve God / (while we can). (IIB5 and V)
(They don't think) / I ought to go home with my father.
(They think) / I should do everything / (what's right).
I hope / I don't have to get used to this place.

DENIAL OF FEELINGS, ATTITUDES, BEHAVIOR, OR MENTAL STATE OF THE SELF, EITHER REGARDING THE SELF OR OTHERS (IIC)

At times, the denial score IIC is given to a clause which is not verbalized using a negative (as are most denials) but is so clearcut an example of denial within the context that it is coded. The last several examples below are illustrative of this.

(When I fell off) / it didn't discourage me from going back up. (IIB1*b* and IIC)
I never crimed or aided any criminal work. (IIIA3 and IIC)
I'm not too nervous any more.
I don't have any troubles.
I didn't feel like getting into an argument.
(I don't see) / that there's anything wrong with me. (IIB4 and IIC)
I have no complaints.
I'm not scared or anything.
We never did fight.
There's no reason for me to be in a hospital. (IIC and IIB1*b*)
I'm not afraid of steps no more.
I don't have to work.
That don't bother me now.
Nothing is weak about me.
(I said) / why, Mother, that ain't foolish.
I don't mind it so much.
I never wanted to possess anyone.
I never had any trouble with anyone.

THE "SCHIZOPHRENIC" SCALE   151

I don't like tearing up windows.
I was just kidding them / (when I threw rocks at them). (IIC and IB1)
And I sure enjoyed it working day and night. (IIB3 and IIC)
(My brother hit me and pushed me) / I always got along well with my brother. (IB2 and IIC)
(Scrubbing floors is awful hard). / It's real nice though. (IIB1*b* and IIC)

REFERENCES TO FOOD (IID)

Bad, dangerous, unpleasant, or otherwise negative; interferences or delays in eating; too much and wish to have less; too little and wish to have more (IID1)

He wasn't hungry.
The food had a white scum on it.
I gulped my food.
(They asked me) / why I won't eat.
Tomatoes make me break out.
Their food is never served warm enough.
Their food is dull.
They always have too much starchy stuff.
I could hardly touch that mound of food.
I haven't had anything to eat since breakfast.

Good or neutral, pleasant, positive (IID2)

They baked pies that day.
I had dinner in the dining room.
I like the food at home.
He took a loaf of bread to feed the bears.
We stopped for pop and stuff like that.
They are going to bring ice cream and cake.
I'll feed myself.
I ate lots of raw carrots.
It's time for our coffee.
We stopped at a wayside place for a snack.
After I eat breakfast / (I go back upstairs).

REFERENCES TO WEATHER (IIE)

Bad, dangerous, unpleasant, or otherwise negative (not sunny, not clear, uncomfortable, etc.) (IIE1)

The heat makes everything seem sticky.
It's raining outside.
It'll soon be a hot weekend.
It has not been a nice August.

That wind is really cold.
It looks like another dreary, cloudy day.
I'm sick of this awful heat.
This weather is too cold.
It looks like another gray winter day.
It's been a miserable winter.
The humidity must be higher than usual.
We need rain badly.

Good, pleasant, neutral (IIE2)

It was a bright day.
This is the first real day of spring.
The snow was so pretty.
The rain makes a nice sound.
It's another nice day today.
I will listen to the weather report.
These fall days are so crisp and invigorating.
(I dreamed) / the sun was shining on me.
It's a beautiful day for a picnic.

REFERENCES TO SLEEP (IIF)

Bad, dangerous, unpleasant, or otherwise negative; too much; too little (IIF1)

I couldn't get back to sleep.
I woke up from a bad dream.
Every night, I wake up and sit for a few hours.
I had to carry a very sleepy kid.
We fell asleep quite anxiously.
I lay awake for hours.
We didn't do much sleeping that night.
I didn't sleep a wink last night.
Going to sleep bothers me.
I can't sleep in a hospital bed.
I still have nightmares.
I can't seem to stay awake enough.
Trying to get to sleep is an agony.

Good, pleasant, or neutral (IIF2)

I have good dreams sometimes.
I sleep till one o'clock.
I go to sleep right after the news report.
I awoke feeling refreshed.
I sleep good at night.
It was a lovely nap.
I go to bed at night.

References to Disorganization and Repetition (III)

The third major subdivision of the Social Alienation–Personal Disorganization (Schizophrenic) Scale includes three types of signs of disorganization and two kinds of repetitive speech.

SIGNS OF DISORGANIZATION (IIIA)

Remarks or words that are not understandable or are inaudible (IIIA1)

The most literal interpretation of this subcategory leading to a code of IIIA1 occurs at all points in the verbal sample where the typescript indicates that words have been omitted because the typist could not make them out. Our typescripts show the approximate number of words omitted in parentheses, and each such indication of omitted words is scored IIIA1. If the typist has included extraneous noises which may have caused the inaudibility, a decision may be made by the content coder *not* to score IIIA1. Consider the following example: "I went with my father (three words omitted—sound of telephone ringing masks the speaker's words) at that time." In this instance one does not code IIIA1 since it seems clear that the lack of audibility is due to circumstances beyond the speaker's control.

A second use of this content category (IIIA1) is in those instances where the terms "illogical," "bizarre," or "erroneous" are too strong, but where the lexical content does not quite "make sense." In these cases also we have employed the categorization of disorganization (IIIA1) in the sense that the coder cannot understand what is being said.

Examples of both kinds of interpretation of the category IIIA1 are given below.

OMITTED OR INAUDIBLE WORDS:

The thing of it is (2 words) all right.
I go down to the room and (5 words omitted   ).
Well, I guess (approximately 6 words   ) okay.

REMARKS THAT ARE NOT UNDERSTANDABLE:

(I haven't made any plans) / and everyday to live.
Tomorrow is Friday / I guess all day.
The crust is real black on the trees.
(I had my shower today.) / I'm for blowing bubbles.

(My sister agreed to go to a sanitarium.) / She was consulted by many psychiatrists.
Only the nurse, she gives me one. (Nothing in context serves as referent.)
My life's getting older.
Love inspires, despires, and leads the way.
The gadicator isn't working.
That's loud enough to be noiging.
The flowers are froggy.

Incomplete sentences, clauses, phrases; blocking (IIIA2)

Two categories of incomplete statements or signs of blocking are coded IIIA2. In the first, there are various degrees of breaking off of a word or idea. This is sometimes accompanied by a resumption of the same word or idea and sometimes followed by the introduction of a new topic. A second category of incomplete sentences or clauses is that which results when the subject completely omits grammatically necessary words.

VARIOUS DEGREES OF BREAKING OFF OF A WORD OR IDEA:

She lives in a little in Pine Spring, Georgia.
But I . . . they . . . it may be that . . .
I had good spectacles. / I just uh that fine print.
We went to uh / her neighbors were there.
I have a oh / anyway that's it.
When he gave me that job down in the . . . / I was there in April.
About the best experience and greatest is / when they . . . since I've been here.
(We have an Edison phonograph) / (that my father bought) / and it had of course at that time / (that was around 1920 / I think).

COMPLETE OMISSION OF GRAMMATICALLY NECESSARY WORDS:

At . . . I went upstairs.
I went to . . . / anyway when I left.
I didn't . . . / that would start happening again.
As far as I . . . well, I'm willing to cooperate.
They . . . one of them had a boy.
There was / there . . . when we did go out. (IIIB1 and IIIA2)
You pu . . . put the sealing pu . . . pu . . .

Obviously erroneous or fallacious remarks or conclusions; illogical or bizarre statements (IIIA3)

There are fifty small things in my mind.
I watch them pool / (I mean bowl).
(I cannot die) / because they put too much energy under me.
It'll act like a tray. (In illogical context.)

The ray inside of me tells them what to do.
I lived on another star for 10,000 years.
My grandmother's the only way / (I know).
(Whatever is the answer) / is a backward concern.
(I think) / the secret fluid of the body is stuff to hurt you. (IIIA3 and IB2)
The last tooth // I had pulled // had a big cavity; / must have been born that way or something. (IIB1*a* and IIIA3)
Every feeling of the soul should be heavenborn, earthborn, and hellborn.
That nurse there drives me away to being dead and that. (IIIA3 and IA2)
(Let's see) / quinine capsules and running around on the streets and that.
Tortured truth is all mashed up and down.
Lots of capsules, capital, capsule and pyramids, summits, cobbets, robbets, jobbets, robadobets, subbets, cubbets, robbets.
(The white scum that comes on my teeth / I don't know) / if it's fermenting from my ear. (IIIA3 and IIB4)
I've been losing friends by these rays incriminating. (IIIA3 and IA2)
(When I turn my head) / it seems like a blaze upon me.
I prayed for the world to get up as possibly as good / as they can.
Do you think babies have the right idea / and people have the wrong idea? (IIIA3 and IVA)
I have an atomic personality. / My brain is atomic. / My skin is atomic. (Three codings of IIIA3)
I'm on the intake side instead of a government introducer.
I make use of my magnetic background with people and heredities.
Thought was an erasure of father's shocked by his chronic conversation.
That was my method to get close to the patient and a deep down-to-earth sincerity in your inflection / (as though you were walking through a dog kennel).

REPETITION OF WORDS OR OF IDEAS (IIIB)

Since the coding of this category requires that one focus on structure rather completely, we have found that it may be easier to code both IIIB1 and IIIB2 separately rather than in conjunction with the rest of the scale. Our procedure has been to carry out the coding of all categories but IIIB1 and IIIB2 and then to reread the verbal sample looking only for codable repetitions.

Repetition of words separated by no more than a word (IIIB1).

Exclude instances due to grammatical and syntactical convention where words are repeated, for example, "as far as," "by and by," and so forth; also, exclude instances where such words as "I" and "the" are separated by a word. Contractions are regarded as single linguistic units. Repetitions are italicized below and in coded samples at end of chapter.

> Well, *one, one* experience I had.
> *I, I, I,* was going to the show. (Two scores IIIB1 are given.)
> That's *all.* / *All* is true.
> *That's* / *that's* something to think about.
> I *do* that / *do* radio repair work.
> I *get* well *get* my voice on this tape.
> I had that done *in* the *in* a machine shop.
> *You, you* get a bed at least.
> I feel *awful* bad, *awful* helpless. (IIIB1 and IIB1*b*)

Repetition of ideas in sequence.—Repetition of phrases or clauses separated by no more than a phrase or a clause (IIIB2)

> *I'd like* / *I'd like* it.
> *He went sliding in* the snow. / There was snow on the roof / and *he went sliding in* it.
> I just *don't feel* all right. / I *don't feel* right. (IIIB2 and IIB1c for each clause)
> *They tried* to go / and *they tried* to get me to go.
> If you *make three progressions, make three progressions* / you could win. (IIIB2 and ID2)
> *A scientist could* do that / I always thought / only *a scientist could* find anything there.
> *I been* / *I been* mopping and sweeping.
> We're on two-thirds of *the winter* / *the winter* isn't the worst.
> *I like* the shade and the flowers / *I like* to be doing something.
> I didn't do much *this week* / but *this week* was pretty slow.
> They had *a little, a little* poem.
> What's *he going to* do with it? / *He's going to* use it.
> *Now I guess* / it's about 10:15 / *now, I guess.*
> *I could go* / *I could go* with you.
> *He don't* / *he don't* furnish coffee.
> I ain't one of them / that *like to do* a lot of talking / I *like to do* some work.
> *I been trying to* do it / like he said / *I been trying to* get there.

Questions or Other References Directed to the Interviewer (IV)

QUESTIONS (IVA)

> What do you want?
> Will that do?

Should I go on?
Do I have to talk? (IVA and IIB5)
Is the five minutes up?
Were you here before?

OTHER REFERENCES (IVB)

I never met you before.
(When I was there) / you know / (before you came).
(It was like this) / you see . . .
(I think) / you are a new doctor.
Excuse me, doctor.

Religious and Biblical References (V)

In the past, this category has been given a literal interpretation, and all references of whatever kind to any religious or biblical subject matter were scored. We now distinguish whether religious or biblical references pertain to the self or are, in effect, statements about religion as an institution. Another way of making the distinction is in the separation of the mystical from the habitual in references to religion. That is, one may make secular statements about a sacred institution in the same sense that such statements are made about nonsacred institutions. For example, the statement "I went to church yesterday" may not have much difference in meaning to the speaker from "I went to a play yesterday." When a person is emphasizing the meaning of religion for himself, the statement is to be coded.

Another cue to use in distinguishing references to be coded in the category of religious and biblical references (V) are those which indicate unusual or deviant uses of religious rituals, for example, "I go to confession frequently," "I went to church daily," or "I prayed all night." References indicative of turning to religion as regression or as an expression of a need for security should be coded. Code *only* statements regarding the self unless the clause is embedded in a context where the self is clearly involved.

I just keep praying.
That explains my deep interest in religion all my life.
My interest in religion has been important.
My best experiences have been in religion.
We do what God wants us to do. (V and IIB5)
I had dreams of the Lord.
I really took the Lord for my Saviour.
The Lord watches over me. (V and IC3)

Prayers helped me / when I was hospitalized. (V and IIB1c)
We have to be true in serving the Lord. (IIB5 and V)
I began to think about religion.
It makes you think of some higher power.
I needed God.
I was baptized again.
I really did find God.
Only God can help me. (V and IC3)
I have found the right religion for me.

Verbal Sample # 1 Coded for Schizophrenia

Name of Subject:
   (State hospital patient)
Date:
Name of Study:

Interviewer:
Total Words: 123
Correction Factor: 0.8130

        IIB4   IIB4
Well, I don't know what to start. / I got nothing to say. / Just . . .
    IIB1c   IIIB2   IIB1c
I don't feel [2] all right. / *I don't feel* r . . . / I feel *awful* bad. / . . .
  IIIB1   IIBb1   IIB4   IIB1b
Awful helpless. / I never get to walk. / I'm always the same. / *I never*
          IIIB2   IIB1b   IIB4   IIIB2
change. / *I never* get better. / I don't know *what to* . . . sa . . . *what to*
  IIB1c   IVA   IIIA1
do. / What is the matter with me anyhow? / (2 words) always ask
                 IIIB2   IIB1c   IIIB2   IIB1c
me / if I can walk. / But I *can't* uh I *can't stand*. / *Can't stand* on my
            IIB1c   IIB1c
feet. / I'm getting worse all the time. / It's always worse. / What are
        IVA   IIB1c   IVA   IIIB2 IIB1b
they gonna do with me / *if I* don't get no better? / *If I* stay the
  IVA   IIB4   IVA
same? / I don't know what to say. / What do they call this? / Why
  IIB5   IVA
do you make me do this? /

---

[2] Repetitions are italicized.

THE "SCHIZOPHRENIC" SCALE 159

SCHIZOPHRENIC SCALE SHEET

Study _____   Scorer _____

                                Words 123   C.F. 0.8130

Identification Subject # 1   Date _____

Category	Tally	Total	Weighted score	Percent score
IA1	....	....	....	....
A2	....	....	....	....
IB1	....	....	....	....
B2	....	....	....	....
IC1	....	....	....	....
C2	....	....	....	....
C3	....	....	....	....
ID1	....	....	....	....
D2	....	....	....	....
IIA	....	....	....	....
IIB1a	....	....	....	....
B1b	....	4	+4	....
B1c	....	8	0	....
B2	....	....	....	....
B3a	....	....	....	....
B3b	....	....	....	....
B4	....	5	+2½	....
B5	....	1	+½	....
IIC	....	....	....	....
IID1	....	....	....	....
D2	....	....	....	....
IIE1	....	....	....	....
E2	....	....	....	....
IIF1	....	....	....	....
F2	....	....	....	....
IIIA1	....	1	+1	....
A2	....	....	....	....
A3	....	....	....	....
IIIB1	....	1	0	....
B2	....	6	+6	....
IVA	....	6	+6	....
IVB	....	....	....	....
V	....	....	....	....
Totals	....	....	+20	....

Corrected score = total weighted score × C.F. = +16.26

Verbal Sample # 2 Coded for Schizophrenia

Name of Subject:
  (State hospital patient)
Date:
Name of Study:

Interviewer:
Total Words: 130
Correction Factor: 0.7692

        IIIB1   IIIB1
Well, I stayed home with my mother *all all all*[3] the time. / I never
  IIB1*b*   IVA   IIB5   IIIA1
went out / unless she went too. / Is that all right? / (3 words
                         IA2
omitted) Never had no boy friends to go out with. / *Every place*
   IIIB2   IIIB2   IIIA2
every place I went / why *I went* with my mother. / There wa . . . /
                                    IIIA2
And another couple went along. / They . . . / One of 'em had a boy
                     IIIB2   IIB5
with them. / *They tried* . . . / *they tried* to get me to go with him. /
         IA1   IIB4
But I wouldn't go with anybody. / Hm. I don't know / *When I* do /
    IIIB2   IC2
when I did go out / and we had a party or something / they was
    IB2   IC1   IIIA2   IIB1*b*
always kidding me. / Now she's married / and now I, here I set. /
   IIB3*a*   IIB1*b*
And I was lucky cause / I didn't get married. / I got *my mother* / . . .
  IIIB2   IC3
had *my mother* yet. /

---

[3] Repetitions are italicized.

SCHIZOPHRENIC SCALE SHEET

Study _____   Scorer _____

                                                                  Words 130   C.F. 0.7692

Identification Subject # 2   Date _____

Category	Tally	Total	Weighted score	Percent score
IA1	....	1	0	....
A2	....	1	+1	....
IB1	....	....	....	....
B2	....	1	+⅓	....
IC1	....	1	−2	....
C2	....	1	−2	....
C3	....	1	−2	....
ID1	....	....	....	....
D2	....	....	....	....
IIA	....	....	....	....
IIB1a	....	....	....	....
B1b	....	3	+3	....
B1c	....	....	....	....
B2	....	....	....	....
B3a	....	1	−1	....
B3b	....	....	....	....
B4	....	1	+½	....
B5	....	2	+1	....
IIC	....	....	....	....
IID1	....	....	....	....
D2	....	....	....	....
IIE1	....	....	....	....
E2	....	....	....	....
IIF1	....	....	....	....
F2	....	....	....	....
IIIA1	....	1	+1	....
A2	....	3	0	....
A3	....	....	....	....
IIIB1	....	2	0	....
B2	....	5	+5	....
IVA	....	1	+1	....
IVB	....	....	....	....
V	....	....	....	....
Totals	....	....	+5⅚	....

Corrected score = total weighted score × C.F. = +2.50

THE "SCHIZOPHRENIC" SCALE

Verbal Sample # 3 Coded for Schizophrenia

Name of Subject:
  (State hospital patient)   Interviewer:
Date: Total Words: 200
Name of Study: Correction Factor: 0.5000

      IIB1*b*   IA2
Well, rather a heartache. / My husband ran off with another woman. /
    IIB1*b*   IA2   IIIA2
It broke up my home. / And he took the boy from me / so that he
              IB2
co . . . / Would put me out in the asylum in other words. / But it
  ID1   ID1   IVB
didn't work. / My son learned to drink and everything else at age
                    ID1
sixteen, doctor. / And then he ran off / before he got his diploma /
  IC1   IVB   ID1
and got married, doctor. / Which turned my father forever, / I
        IIB1*b*   IIB5   IA1
think / that's the most prominent tragedy for me. / Because *I have*
  IC2   IIIB2   IIB5   IA1
to[4] divorce him loving him just the same. / *I have to* get the di-
                   IA1   ID1
vorce. / And it's made it hard for the boy to get along. / Between
  IIIA3   IVA
the two both living. / Did you want to know something about com-
      IIB1*b*   IIB1*c*   IVB
ing in here? / I was overworked / the year they brought me in here,
      IIB1*b*   IIB3*b*
doctor. / I had a nervous breakdown. / I did all right / till my teeth
     IIIA3   IIB5
came into the evidence foreground. / But I've always obeyed every
          IIB5   IIB4
order / that has been put in front of me. / *I couldn't get a job* / if I
        IIIB2   IIB4   IA2
wanted one / *I couldn't get a job* at my age. / They don't take old
   IVB   IIB5
people / you know. / I sort of feel / I should do / what the hospital
says. /

---

[4] Repetitions are italicized.

SCHIZOPHRENIC SCALE SHEET

Study _____   Scorer _____

                                  Words 200   C.F. 0.5000

Identification Subject # 3   Date _____

Category	Tally	Total	Weighted score	Percent score
IA1	....	3	0	....
A2	....	3	+3	....
IB1	....	....	....	....
B2	....	1	+⅓	....
IC1	....	1	−2	....
C2	....	1	−2	....
C3	....	....	....	....
ID1	....	5	0	....
D2	....	....	....	....
IIA	....	....	....	....
IIB1*a*	....	....	....	....
B1*b*	....	5	+5	....
B1*c*	....	1	0	....
B2	....	....	....	....
B3*a*	....	....	....	....
B3*b*	....	1	−1	....
B4	....	2	+1	....
B5	....	5	+2½	....
IIC	....	....	....	....
IID1	....	....	....	....
D2	....	....	....	....
IIE1	....	....	....	....
E2	....	....	....	....
IIF1	....	....	....	....
F2	....	....	....	....
IIIA1	....	....	....	....
A2	....	1	0	....
A3	....	2	+4	....
IIIB1	....	....	....	....
B2	....	2	+2	....
IVA	....	1	+1	....
IVB	....	4	+2	....
V	....	....	....	....
Totals	....	....	+15⅚	....

Corrected score = total weighted score × C.F. = +7.92

Verbal Sample # 4 Coded for Schizophrenia

Name of Subject:
  (Medical inpatient)
Date:
Name of Study:

Interviewer:
Total Words: 200
Correction Factor: 0.5000

                IIB3a   IIB1c
Well, the best thing ever happened to me / since I been in this hos-
    IIB1c   IIB1a   IC3
pital / when I came here / I was sick and sore / and they worked on
        IC3   IC3
me / *and they operated on* [5] my head. / They put a tube in my leg. /
  IIIB2 IC3   IIB2   IIB3b
And they operated on me / and I feel better. / And I could walk /
               IIB3b   V   IC3
and I'm still walking by the help of the good Lord and the doc-
        IIB3b   IIB3b
tors. / I'm doing all right. / And so I can do most everything / I
   IIB1a   IVB   IIB3b
did / before I taken sick / you know. / I can get up, walk, sing. / I
                                                  IIB3b
like to get up singing, happy, every morning. / And I do that. /
       IIC   IC3
I don't worry them about going home. / They sure have did me
                                                      IC2
good. / And I hope / I continue to feel better. / And I thank the
   V   IC3   IC2
Lord and my doctors for helping me. / I got confidence in them. /
           IIB5   IIIB1 IIB5   IIC
I agree / with anything they say to *do.* / I *do* it. / I don't care /
                        IIC   IIB5
what it is. / I didn't come out here to give orders, / I came out to
          IIB1a
take them. / And so I'm sick / and I want to get better. / And I be-
                      IC3   IIB3a
lieve / they're doing / all they can for me. / I know / 'cause I feel so good. /

---

[5] Repetitions are italicized.

SCHIZOPHRENIC SCALE SHEET

Study _____ Scorer _____

                                                                             Words 200   C.F. 0.5000

Identification Subject # 4   Date _____

Category	Tally	Total	Weighted score	Percent score
IA1				
A2				
IB1				
B2				
IC1				
C2		2	−4	
C3		8	−16	
ID1				
D2				
IIA				
IIB1a		3	0	
B1b				
B1c		2	0	
B2		1	−2	
B3a		2	−2	
B3b		6	−6	
B4				
B5		3	+1½	
IIC		3	+6	
IID1				
D2				
IIE1				
E2				
IIF1				
F2				
IIIA1				
A2				
A3				
IIIB1		1	0	
B2		1	+1	
IVA				
IVB		1	+½	
V		2	+2	
Totals			−19	

Corrected score = total weighted score × C.F. = −9.50

Verbal Sample # 5 Coded for Schizophrenia

Name of Subject:
  (Psychiatric outpatient)   Interviewer:
Date: Total Words: 205
Name of Study: Correction Factor: 0.4878

                IC1   IA1
I'm going to discuss my marriage at 19. / I ran away to (town) /
                  IIB3*b*
one month after I graduated from high school, / and was secretly
            IC1
married for two months. / And then my parents found out / and we
IC2   IC3
tried to make a go of it. / And then I persuaded my husband to trans-
                                  IC2
fer to (Name) University / so I could get a job and support us. /
   IC3   IIB1*b*
Before that his mother had supported us / which created many problems. / When we moved to the university / I got a job for one month
           IIB3*b*
without any typing training. / However, I went to school for a
                                         IB2
week, / so I was trained as a key-punch operator. / *I was fired from* [6]
                     IIB3*b*
my job. / And then I worked for a bank doing clerical work for
            IIIB2   IB2   IA1
about a week. / *I was fired from* that job / because I was absent from
                  IB1   IIB3*b*
work quite a bit / because I hated it. / *Then I worked* for a clothing
                        IA1   IIIB2
store for about a month. / I walked off that job, / and *then I worked*
  IIB3*b*   IIB3*a*
in a little shop / which I enjoyed very much. / Then I played the
                  IIB3*b*   IA1
piano for a dance class for about a month. / Then I left my husband
                             IB1
in September / and came home / and got a divorce from him. /

---

[6] Repetitions are italicized.

SCHIZOPHRENIC SCALE SHEET

Study _____   Scorer _____

Words 205   C.F. 0.4878

Identification Subject # 5   Date _____

Category	Tally	Total	Weighted score	Percent score
IA1	....	4	0	....
A2	....	....	....	....
IB1	....	2	+2	....
B2	....	2	+⅔	....
IC1	....	2	−4	....
C2	....	2	−4	....
C3	....	2	−4	....
ID1	....	....	....	....
D2	....	....	....	....
IIA	....	....	....	....
IIB1a	....	....	....	....
B1b	....	1	+1	....
B1c	....	....	....	....
B2	....	....	....	....
B3a	....	1	−1	....
B3b	....	6	−6	....
B4	....	....	....	....
B5	....	....	....	....
IIC	....	....	....	....
IID1	....	....	....	....
D2	....	....	....	....
IIE1	....	....	....	....
E2	....	....	....	....
IIF1	....	....	....	....
F2	....	....	....	....
IIIA1	....	....	....	....
A2	....	....	....	....
A3	....	....	....	....
IIIB1	....	....	....	....
B2	....	2	+2	....
IVA	....	....	....	....
IVB	....	....	....	....
V	....	....	....	....
Totals	....	....	−13⅓	....

Corrected score = total weighted score × C.F. = −6.49

168   THE "SCHIZOPHRENIC" SCALE

Verbal Sample # 6 Coded for Schizophrenia

Name of Subject:
   (Psychiatric outpatient)   Interviewer:
Date: Total Words: 235
Name of Study: Correction Factor: 0.4253

                                ID1
See / I went to (town) to a funeral, to my uncle's funeral. / And
           IIB1*b*   IIC   IIIB2
I was [7] kind of upset and everything. / I wasn't at first. / *I was* glad
   IC2   ID1
to see my cousin. / And then when they got ready for the funeral /
  IIC   ID1
I didn't realize / until I went up to see the body / that I got real
     IIB1*b*   IIB1*b*   IIB1*b*
upset and started crying / and I couldn't stop. / I felt real sick, nerv-
             IIB1*c*   IID1
ous / and my stomach was upset. / I didn't have any appetite / and
  IIF1
couldn't sleep. / Then when we got ready to leave / I didn't want to
                     IC2
go. / I wanted to stay and help my aunt. / But when I had called
      IIB4   IIIA2   IIB4
her / I didn't know. / I knew / let's see / I didn't know. / I had called
                  IC2
down there / to see how she was / *and then I wrote her a* card, /
           IIIB2   IIIB2
and then I wrote her a letter, / *and then I* sent her a picture of the
                                     IIB1*b*
kids. / And *I was* kind of worried and everything, / because *I*
           IIIB2   IIIB2   IIB1*c*
thought / that *I was* pregnant, / and *I thought,* / that I had lost the
              IIB1*b*   ID1
baby. / Because I was always scared to go to a funeral. / When I got
       IIB1*b*   IIB1*b*
there / I had to break down / because I couldn't hold it in. / And
           IIIA1
then the horn started honking / and my father honked it two times /
                            IIIA3
and *that's why* / I was scared of hearing the horns and everything. /
  IIIB2   IIIA3
That's why / I was glad / they started blowing again today. /

---

[7] Repetitions are italicized.

SCHIZOPHRENIC SCALE SHEET

Study _____   Scorer _____

Words 235   C.F. 0.4253

Identification Subject # 6   Date _____

Category	Tally	Total	Weighted score	Percent score
IA1				
A2				
IB1				
B2				
IC1				
C2		3	−6	
C3				
ID1		4	0	
D2				
IIA				
IIB1*a*				
B1*b*		8	+8	
B1*c*		2	0	
B2				
B3*a*				
B3*b*				
B4		2	+1	
B5				
IIC		2	+6	
IID1		1	0	
D2				
IIE1				
E2				
IIF1		1	0	
F2				
IIIA1		1	+1	
A2		1	0	
A3		2	+4	
IIIB1				
B2		6	+6	
IVA				
IVB				
V				
Totals			+20	

Corrected score = total weighted score × C.F. = +8.51

BIBLIOGRAPHY

Barcus, F. E. Communications content: Analysis of the research, 1900–1958. Unpublished Ph.D. dissertation, University of Illinois, 1959.

Beck, A. T., C. H. Ward, M. Mendelson, J. Mock, and J. Erbaugh. An inventory for measuring depression, *Arch. Gen. Psychiat.*, 4: 561–571, 1961.

Berelson, B. *Content Analysis in Communication Research.* Glencoe, Ill.: The Free Press, 1952.

Bowlby, J. Separation anxiety, *Int. J. Psychoanal.*, 41: 89–113, 1960.

Buss, A. H. *The Psychology of Aggression.* New York: John Wiley and Sons, Inc., 1961.

Cartwright, D. P. Analysis of Qualitative Material, in *Research Methods in the Behavioral Sciences*, pp. 421–470, ed. L. Festinger and D. Katz. New York: The Dryden Press, 1953.

Colby, K. M. Experiments on the effects of an observer's presence on the imago system during psychoanalytic free-association, *Behav. Sci.*, 5: 216–232, 1960.

Dollard, J., and F. Auld, Jr. *Scoring Human Motives: A Manual.* New Haven: Yale University Press, 1959.

Dunphy, D. C. Content analysis—development and critical issues. Unpublished paper, Harvard University, 1964.

Freud, S. *The Problem of Anxiety.* New York: W. W. Norton and Co., Inc., 1936.

Gottschalk, L. A., and G. Hambidge, Jr. Verbal behavior analysis: A systematic approach to the problem of quantifying psychologic processes, *J. Proj. Techn.*, 19: 387–409, 1955.

Gottschalk, L. A., K. J. Springer, and G. C. Gleser. Experiments with a Method of Assessing the Variations in Intensity of Certain Psychological States Occurring During Two Psychotherapeutic Interviews, ch. 7, in *Comparative Psycholinguistic Analysis of Two Psychotherapeutic Interviews*, ed. L. A. Gottschalk. New York: International Universities Press, 1961.

Gottschalk, L. A., S. M. Kaplan, G. C. Gleser, and C. M. Winget. Variations in magnitude of emotion: A method applied to anxiety and hostility during phases of the menstrual cycle, *Psychosom. Med.*, 24: 300–311, 1962.

Gottschalk, L. A., G. C. Gleser, and K. J. Springer. Three hostility scales applicable to verbal samples, *Arch. Gen. Psychiat.*, 9: 254–279, 1963.

Gottschalk, L. A., and G. C. Gleser. Distinguishing Characteristics of the Verbal Communications of Schizophrenic Patients, in *Disorders of Communication A.R.N.M.D.*, 42:400–413. Baltimore: William and Wilkins, 1964.

Gottschalk, L. A., C. M. Winget, G. C. Gleser, and K. J. Springer. The Measurement of Emotional Changes During a Psychiatric Interview. A Working Model Toward Quantifying the Psychoanalytic Concept of Affect, in *Methods of Research in Psychotherapy*, pp. 93–126, ed. L. A. Gottschalk and A. H. Auerbach. New York: Appleton-Century-Crofts, 1966a.

Gottschalk, L. A., W. N. Stone, G. C. Gleser, and J. M. Iacono. Anxiety levels in dreams: Relation to changes in plasma free fatty acids, *Science*, 153: 654–657, 1966b.

Gottschalk, L. A., and G. C. Gleser. *The Measurement of Psychological States Through the Content Analysis of Verbal Behavior.* Berkeley and Los Angeles: University of California Press, 1969.

Hafner, A. J., and A. M. Kaplan. Hostility content analysis of the Rorschach and TAT, *J. Proj. Techn.*, 24: 137–143, 1960.

Holsti, O. R., J. K. Loomba, and R. C. North. Content Analysis, in *Handbook of Social Psychology*, ed. G. Lindzey and E. Aronson. Cambridge, Mass.: Addison-Wesley, 1967.

Horney, K. *Our Inner Conflicts, a Constructive Theory of Neurosis*. New York: W. W. Norton and Co., Inc., 1945.

Janis, I. L. The Problem of Validating Content Analysis, in *The Language of Politics: Studies in Quantitative Semantics*, pp. 55–82, ed. H. D. Lasswell and N. C. Leites. New York: George Stewart, Inc., 1949.

Kaplan, A. Content analysis and the theory of signs, *Philosophy of Science*, 10: 230–247, 1943.

Karacan, I., D. R. Goodenough, A. Shapiro, and S. Starker. Erection cycle during sleep in relation to dream anxiety, *Arch. Gen. Psychiat.*, 15: 183–189, 1966.

Kierkegaard, S. *The Concept of Dread*. Trans. W. Lowrie. Originally published in Danish, 1844. Princeton: Princeton University Press, 1944.

Marsden, G. Content-analysis studies of therapeutic interviews: 1954 to 1964, *Psychol. Bull.*, 68: 298–321, 1965.

Miller, W. B. Lower Class Culture as a Generating Milieu of Gang Delinquency, in *The Sociology of Crime and Delinquency*, ed. M. E. Wolfgang, L. Savity, and N. Johnston. New York: John Wiley, 1962.

Murray, H. A. *Thematic Apperception Test: Manual*. Cambridge, Mass.: Harvard University Press, 1943.

Oken, D. An experimental study of suppressed anger and blood pressure, *A.M.A. Arch. Gen. Psychiat.*, 2: 441–456, 1960.

Osgood, C. E. The Representational Model and Relevant Research Methods, in *Trends in Content Analysis*, pp. 33–38, ed. I. D. Pool. Urbana: University of Illinois Press, 1959.

Piers, G., and M. D. Singer. *Shame and Guilt*. Springfield, Ill.: Charles C Thomas, 1953.

Ross, W. D., N. Adsett, G. C. Gleser, C. R. B. Joyce, S. M. Kaplan and M. E. Tieger. A trial of psychopharmacologic measurement with projective techniques, *J. Proj. Techn.*, 27: 223–225, 1963.

Spitzer, R. L. Immediate available record of mental status exam, *Arch. Gen. Psychiat.*, 13: 76–78, 1965.

Spitzer, R. L., J. L. Fleiss, J. Endicott, and J. Cohen. Mental status schedule: Properties of factor analytically derived scales, *Arch. Gen. Psychiat.*, 16: 479–493, 1967.

Tillich, P. Existential philosophy, *J. Hist. Ideas*, 5: 44–70, 1944.

Winget, C. M. Hostility in the dreams of Negro and white males. Unpublished master's thesis, University of Cincinnati, June, 1967.

Witkin, H. A., and H. B. Lewis. The relation of experimentally induced presleep experiences to dreams: A report on method and preliminary findings, *J. Amer. Psa. Assn.*, 13: 819–849, 1965.

Wittenborn, J. R. *Wittenborn Psychiatric Rating Scales*. New York: The Psychological Corp., 1955.

INDEX OF AUTHORS

Auld, F., Jr., 25

Barcus, F., 2
Berelson, B., 1
Bowlby, J., 40

Cartwright, D., 2
Colby, K., 9

Dollard, J., 25
Dunphy, D., 2

Freud, S., 40, 45

Hafner, A., 16
Hambidge, G., 15
Holsti, O., 2
Horney, K., 35

Janis, I., 1

Kaplan, A., 1, 16
Karacan, I., 15
Kierkegaard, S., 35

Marsden, G., 2
Miller, W., 117
Murray, H., 15

Osgood, C., 2

Piers, G., 45, 49

Rank, O., 40

Singer, M., 45, 49
Spitzer, R., 63

Tillich, P., 35

Winget, C., 15
Witkin, H., 15

INDEX OF SUBJECTS

Abandonment: of self, 41, 119, 121; of others, 43, 68, 77, 85; scoring of, on Hostility Out Scales, 66-67; of animals, 70, 79; scoring of, on Ambivalent Hostility Scales, 116
Abuse, 46, 48
Active voice, 95, 96, 115-116
Affect Scales: scoring of, 21; sample size, 22; correction factor, 21-22; final score, 21-22; tabulation of scores, 21-22
Ambivalent Hostility Scale: def. of, 114; labeling of, 114, 117; weights, 114; listed, 115; number of scores per clause, 115; rules for coding, 115-117; vs. anxiety, 116; color coding, 117; and Hostility In, 117; and Covert Hostility, 117; examples of, 117-122; coded verbal samples, 122-127
Anger: self's, toward others, 69, 74-75; other's, toward others, 78, 84; denial of, 86, 106; self's, toward self, 99-100; other's, toward self, 119
Anxiety Scale: def. of, 29; subtypes of, 29; weights, 30; grammatical tense, 30; assumptions underlying, 30-31; additive properties of, 30-31; fluctuation of scores on, 31; listed, 31; labeling of subtypes, 32; rules for use of, 32-34; clause identification, 35; coded verbal samples for, 54-60
Anxiety coding: speaker as agent of anxiety, 32; use of "we" or "us," 32-33; external source of anxiety, 32; use of weights, 33; number of scores per clause, 33-34; ref. to "bound anxiety," 34; denials of anxiety, 34; use of color in, 34; ref. to suicide, 35-36
Avoidance behavior, 133-135

Beck Depression Inventory, 93
Birth trauma. See Separation Anxiety
Blame: self's, of others, 69, 74; other's, of others, 78, 83; self's of self, 99; denial of, 106, 121-122; other's, of self, 118
Bound anxiety, 29, 34
Buss Hostility Inventory, 63

Cancer, 36
Castration Anxiety. See Mutilation Anxiety
Clauses: as coding unit, 11-12; method of notating, 23; with elliptical subject or predicate, 23; identification of, 23-24, 35, 131; examples of, 24; parenthetical, 24; effect of context on, 25; grammatical tense of, 27, 30, 131, 141,

173

Clauses (*continued*) 146, 147; number of scores within, 27, 33-34, 65, 115, 132, 137; with multiple objects, 65; with series of verbs, 65; series within, 132; repetition of, 156
Coding unit, 25-26. *See also* Clauses
Color coding, 34, 67, 97, 117
Condemnation, 46-47, 48
Consistency of scores, 17, 31
Construct validity, 62-63
Content Analysis, 1-2
Context, 97, 115-116, 142
Correction factor, 10, 14, 21-22
Covert Hostility: def. of, 62; labeling of, 63; examples of, 75-86; denial of, 86; coded verbal samples for, 86-92
Covert Hostility scoring ref. to: killing, 75, 78, 80-81, 82, 85, 86; anger, 75, 78, 84; fighting, 76; robbing, 76-77, 79, 82, 85; injuries, 76, 78-79, 81, 82, 84-85; criticism, 77, 78, 79, 83; suffering, 77, 79, 85. *See also* Hostility Directed Outward
Criticism: self's, of self, 46, 102; self's, of others, 47-48, 68-69, 71, 73; other's, of others, 77, 79, 83; other's, of self, 118
Cursing, 75, 84

Death: of others, 67, 75, 80-81, 85, 86; of animals, 70, 72, 78, 81; of self, 98, 117, 121
Death anxiety: rules for scoring, 35-36; ref. to self, 36-37; examples of, 36-38; ref. to animate others, 37; ref. to inanimate others, 37-38; denial of, 38. *See also* Anxiety Scale
Deficiencies, 50-52
Denial: of anxiety, 34, 38, 40, 44, 48, 52, 54; of anger, 86, 106; of destructive impulses, 106; of blame, 106, 121-122
Desertion, 41, 43, 143-144
Despair, 101
Destruction: of inanimate objects, 72-73; of flora, 72-73, 82; of wildlife, 72-73, 82
Diffuse Anxiety: def. of, 52-53; use of "trouble" in, 52; use of "uncomfortable" in, 52-53; use of "bother" in, 53; ref. to others anxious, 53; ref. to self anxious, 53; examples of, 53-54; denial of, 54; word forms in, 60-61; scorable words listed for, 60-61. *See also* Anxiety Scale
Disappointment, 71-72, 80, 104, 105, 120
Disapproval, 47, 48
Discouragement, 100
Diseases, 36

Disorganization, 153-156
Disorientation, 141-142
Dissociation, 144-145
Dreams, 15, 27-28
Embarrassment, 50, 51, 96
Environment, 7
Equipment for obtaining samples, 7
Errors in coding, 19
Examples: of clausing, 24; of Death Anxiety, 36-38; of Mutilation Anxiety, 38-40; of Separation Anxiety, 41-44; of Guilt Anxiety, 45-48; of Shame Anxiety, 49-52; of Diffuse Anxiety, 53-54; of Overt Hostility, 67-75; of Hostility Directed Outward, 67-86; of Covert Hostility, 75-86; of Hostility Directed Inward, 97-107; of Ambivalent Hostility, 117-122; of interpersonal references, 132-141

Falling, 42, 44
Fantasies, 27-28
Fighting, 67, 76
Fishing, 36
Food, 151
Friendliness, 137-139
Funerals, 35

Generalized others, 28, 66
Grammatical tense of clauses, 27, 30, 131, 141, 146, 147
Graveyards, 35
Guilt Anxiety: def. of, 45; source of, 45; examples of, 45-48; denial of, 48. *See also* Anxiety Scale

Heart attack, 36
Hostility Directed Inward Scale: def. of, 93; weights on, 93-94; listed, 94-95; examples of, 97-107; coded verbal samples for, 107-113
Hostility Directed Inward coding: ref. to outside agents, 95; plural nouns and pronouns, 95; passive voice, 95, 96; self-criticism, 96; importance of context in, 97; conscious vs. unconscious intent, 97; use of color in, 97; ref. to self-destruction, 98-99; ref. to self-depreciation, 102-103; denial of hostility, 106
Hostility Directed Outward Scale: def. of, 62; intensity continuum on, 62; weights on, 62; construct validity for, 62-63; listed, 64-65; rules for coding, 65-67; examples of, 67-86; coded verbal samples, 86-92
Hostility Directed Outward coding: number of scores per clause, 65; use of "we" or "us," 66; use of "you," 66; single words, 66; use of color in, 67

INDEX 175

Humiliation, 50, 51
Hunting, 36

Identification of data, 8
Illness, 67, 143
Inadequacy, 49-50, 51, 144
Inferential meanings, 27, 28
Inferiority feelings. *See* Shame Anxiety
Injury: vs. illness, 67; to others, 67, 76, 84-85, 86; to animals, 70, 72, 78-79, 81, 82; to inanimate objects, 72, 81, 82; to plants, 72, 81; to self, 98-99, 118, 121
Instructions to interviewer, 5, 8
Instructions to subject, 4, 5, 9
Intensity continuum, 62
Interjudge reliability, 17, 18, 31
Interpersonal references, 132-141
Interscorer variance, 27
Interviewer: effects on content, 4, 6; role of, 5; training of, 6; instructions to, 5, 8; absence of, 9; questions directed to, 156-157; comments directed to, 157
Intrapersonal references, 141-152

Labeling: of Anxiety subtypes, 32; of Hostility Outward, 63; of Hostility Inward, 97; of Ambivalent Hostility, 114, 117
Literal meanings, 27, 28
Loneliness, 42-43, 44, 104-105
Longitudinal studies, 131
Love objects, 42, 44

Masochism, 93
Mental Status Schedule, 63
Minnesota Multiphasic Personality Inventory, 63
Mutilation, 99, 118
Mutilation Anxiety: def. of, 38; ref. to self, 38-39; examples of, 38-40; ref. to animate others, 39; ref. to inanimate objects, 39-40; denial of, 40. *See also* Anxiety Scale

Nonspecific Anxiety. *See* Diffuse Anxiety

Oken Hostility Scale, 63, 93
Ostracism, 41, 43
Overt Hostility: def. of, 62; labeling of, 63; examples of, 67-75; coded verbal samples, 86-92
Overt Hostility scoring ref. to: injury, 67, 70, 72; killing, 67, 70, 72; suffering, 68, 70; robbery, 68, 70, 73; criticism, 68-69, 71, 73, 74. *See also* Hostility Directed Outward Scale

Passive voice, 95, 96
Pragmatics, 1-2
Projective tests, 15-16
Pronouns, use of, 26-27, 32-33, 66, 95
Psychotherapeutic Interviews, 15

Quotations, 27-28

Reliability, 20, 26, 128
Religious references, 157-158
Repetition: of words, 155-156; of clauses, 156; of ideas, 156; of phrases, 156
Ridicule, 49
Robbery: self's, of others, 68, 70, 73, 82; other's, of others, 76-77, 79, 85; other's, of self, 119, 121
Rules for coding: Anxiety Scale, 32-34; Hostility Directed Outward Scale, 65-67; Hostility Directed Inward Scale, 95-97; Ambivalent Hostility Scale, 115-117; Schizophrenic Scale, 131-132

Schizophrenic Scale: weights on, 22, 128-129, 131; final score, 22; def. of, 128; scoring reliability, 128; categories of, 129; listed, 129-131; longitudinal studies of, 131; rules for coding, 131-132; examples of, 132-158; importance of context in, 142; coded verbal samples for, 158-169
Schizophrenic Scale coding: ref. to animals, 132; ref. to inanimate objects, 132; avoidance behavior, 133-135; unfriendly behavior, 135-137; friendly behavior, 137-139; negative ref. toward others, 139-140; positive ref. toward others, 139-141; disoriented responses, 141-142; negative ref. toward self, 142-146, 149; positive ref. toward self, 146-148, 149-150; denial of mental state, 150-151; signs of disorganization, 153-156; illogical statements, 154-155; remarks to interviewer, 156-157; religious references, 157-158
Semantics, 1
Semiotics, 1
Separation Anxiety: def. of, 40; ref. to desertion, 41, 43; ref. to abandonment, 41, 43; ref. to ostracism, 41, 43; examples of, 41-44; ref. to loss of support, 42, 43, 44; ref. to loss of love object, 42, 44; ref. to loneliness, 42-43, 44; denial of, 44. *See also* Anxiety Scale
Shame Anxiety: def. of, 49; ref. to ridicule, 49, 51; ref. to inadequacy, 49-50, 51; examples of, 49-52; ref. to embarrassment, 50, 51; ref. to humilia-

Shame Anxiety (*continued*)
  tion, 50, 51; ref. to deficiencies, 50-51, 51-52; denial of, 52
Sleep, 152
Social Alienation–Personal Disorganization Scale. *See* Schizophrenic Scale
Square root transformation, 22
Suicide, 35-36, 97-98
Summarizing unit, 25-26. *See also* Clauses
Syntactics, 1

Technician qualifications, 17
Technician training, 17-18, 19-20
Thematic Apperception Test, 15-16
Transcription of samples, 10

Verbal samples: content of, 5; interviewer for, 6, 8, 9; environment for, 7; equipment for, 7; identification of, 8; typing of, 10-11; written, 16; number of words in, 22; reliability of, 26; coded, 54-60, 86-92, 107-113, 122-127, 158-169

War, 35
Weather, 151-152
Weights: for Schizophrenic Scale, 22, 128-129, 131, 147; for Anxiety Scale, 30, 33; for Hostility Directed Outward Scale, 62; for Hostility Directed Inward Scale, 93-94, 97; for Ambivalent Hostility Scale, 114
Wittenborn Psychiatric Rating Scales, 63, 93
Word Count: for tabulation, 10, 12-14; minimal number for reliability, 15, 20